THE BEST OF
THAI DISHES

by Sisamon Kongpan

SANGDAD PUBLICATIONS

National Library of Thailand Cataloging in Publication Data.
The Best of Thai Dishes--3rd ed.--Bangkok.
Sangdad, 1998.
192 p.
1. Cookery, Thai. I. Title.
641.59593
ISBN: 974-7162-62-8

First Published, 1991 by SANGDAD PUBLISHING CO., LTD
Second Published, 1992 by SANGDAD PUBLISHING CO., LTD
Third Published, 1998 by SANGDAD PUBLISHING CO., LTD

Director Nidda Hongwiwat
Writer Sisamon Kongpan
Photographer Samart Sudto
         Sangwan Phrathep
Design & Layout Samart Sudto
Layout   Rung-Rudee Panichsri
         Pranee Pongpun
Illustration Rung-Rudee Panichsri
Marketing Director Wenisa Chotiaroon
Production Director Jiranan Tubniem

Publisher and Distributor Sangdad Publishing Co., Ltd.
320 Lat Phroa 94 (Town in Town)
Wangthonglang, Bangkok 10310 Thailand
Tel. (662) 538-7576, 538-5553, 538-1499
Fax: (662) 538-1499
Printer Phongwarin Printing Ltd.
Tel. (662) 399-4525-31

Plan of the Book

INTRODUCTION

Thai cooking is an artform. Before I write about the recipes themselves, we need to generate a sense of it s overall process. Maybe the word "rice" creates a definite image or sensation for you. There are hardly any meals served in Thailand where there is not rice. It is the basis of our diet. If you observe "rice" carefully you will see that it has a certain absorbtive quality. It is also very malleable, and easy to store. **It can be dished up quickly** and combined with many dishes, absorbing their flavors. On the dinner table there might be as many as twenty courses of meat, vegetables, fish and fruit dishes, which can be combined in any combination desired with one's rice. In this way, the rice always has the taste of the chosen dish. This is the reason **the Thai are never tired of rice.** The rice and its complimentary dish become one—like yang and yin.

You could say that cooking is like a meditation. One needs to be focused in a calm way in order to surmount the barriers for reaching one's goal of a near-perfect meal. We do not need lopsided and oversized vegetables and bulgy-fatty pieces of meat. Another barrier is the desire to use an over-abundance of spices. It comes from a fear that one will not be able to taste the meal and a mistrust of recipes.

Actually there is considerable skill, know-how and even mythology involved in the cooking process. In Thailand we often use a section of the trunk of a tamarind tree as a chopping block. There are many cooks who believe that this will add to the ultimate flavor of the finished product. It is true

that one cannot be an expert Thai cook without considerable practice at cutting, as well as focusing on the actual process going on in the cooking utensil. The meat should be sliced into even, small or thin pieces. Vegetables are cut at an angle and in much the same way. It seems that every chef has his or her own idiosyncrasies about cutting, but there are some basics that most of us will agree on. We will all agree that fish, for example, is scored (cut slightly sometimes in patterns) just before steaming. This allows the herbs and spieces which garnish the fish to permeate it s flesh. To empower the fish with your own flair and artistery will be a matter of style and focus.

One of the little secrets of our cooking process is the use of spices. Take a coriander seed, for example, it is a small seed about the size of a beebee, and it seems just as hard. If you put the seeds in a dry frying pan or wok, they will roast and become soft. But, then, if one crushes the seed before roasting, one will immediately smell the delicious aroma. If you cook the seeds in a pan that has a little oil eventually the seed will burst and release the flavor. However, the oil may blacken during the time it takes to burst the seeds. This will give your cooking a burnt taste: this is a no-no. It depends on how you want to release the flavor. The same idea applies to almost any seed, which is one of the reasons the mortar and pestle is so popular. Sometimes you will want to crush the seeds for the purpose of making a paste. The important point for cooking seeds is that the heat, whatever type, should be low. As they are being cooked the seeds should be constantly turned. If one has a wok, a large metal spatula that is curved to fit the side of the rounded wok will be used.

The wok is the utensil par exellence for the production, control and distribution of heat. For those who have never seen a wok before, I like to describe it as an upside-down iron hat. Imagine the perimeter of the hat expanded twice the size of your head; take it off and place it on a metal ring on the coals or stove. If you want to buy an authentic wok go to a Thai or any oriental grocery. There are different sizes of woks; choose one that fits your cooking needs.

First of all, the wok needs to be cleaned and dried. This is a very important first step because sometimes the manufacturer coats the metal with a protective substance. The rest is simple: rub both the outside and inside with vegetable oil and then place the wok in an oven at about 350 degrees for around two hours. Then, after turning off the oven, let the wok cool down in the oven the wok has been seasoned, a kind of cooking process in itself. A great reason to have a finely seasoned wok is that you will not have to use as much oil. Season your wok well , and never use more than two tablespoons of oil, and just use common sense in the amount of food you want to cook at the same time.

Steaming is another form of Thai cooking. Once you have decided that this is a good way to cook, you can invest in a steamer. There are metal and bamboo steamer trays. The bamboo ones will fit inside your wok. Because the water and it s steam will remove the layer of seasoning formed on the surface of the wok, it is a little awkward to always have to re-season the utensil. But, you can also purchase metal trays with a seperate steamer pot. They are very practical.

If your steam trays warp or lose their shape they will not fit on top of each other. This is enough to give up steaming. Store the trays in spot where the rims will not be damaged. It is very important to put enough water in your wok. If your water boils away, guess what happens to your wok! Steaming is fun. You can reload your trays over and over

again; all that is needed is a steady stream of steam and plenty of food. Fill your wok or pot at least three-quarters full of water, and do not remove the lid or the trays until you are almost sure the food is done.

Now that you have an insider's look at the meditative process of Thai cooking you are ready for some images of rice, flour, noodles, sugars and so on. This will help you in purchasing your groceries in Thai and other oriental food stores.

RICE

Rice, khao jao, ข้าวเจ้า, the staple food in the central and southern parts of Thailand, is long-grained, nonglutinous rice. Uncooked grains are translucent; when cooked, the rice is white and fluffy.

Glutinous rice, khao niao, ข้าวเหนียว, also known as sticky rice, is the mainstay of the diet in the northern and northeastern regions of the country and is used in confections in all regions. Uncooked grains are starchy white in color.

Fermented rice, khao mak, ข้าวหมาก, is made by fermenting cooked glutinous rice and is sold as a sweet.

Rice-pot crust, khao tang, ข้าวตัง, is the crust which sometimes forms at the bottom of the pot in which rice is cooked. This is dried in the sun. Dried pot crust is available in the market. It is fried before eating.

FLOUR

Rice flour, paeng khao jao, แป้งข้าวเจ้า, is made from nonglutinous rice.

Glutinous rice flour, paeng khao niao, แป้งข้าวเหนียว, is made from glutinous rice.

Corn flour, paeng khao phot, แป้งข้าวโพด, is a fine white flour made from corn.

Tapioca pellets, sa-khu met lek, สาคูเม็ดเล็ก, are the tiny balls (about 2 mm in diameter) made from tapioca, some used in sweets. They should be mixed with hot, but not scalding, water and kneaded, and then allowed to stand for a time covered with a damp cloth to permit the water to penetrate to the core.

Wheat flour, paeng sa-li, แป้งสาลี, may be general purpose flour unless cake flour is specified.

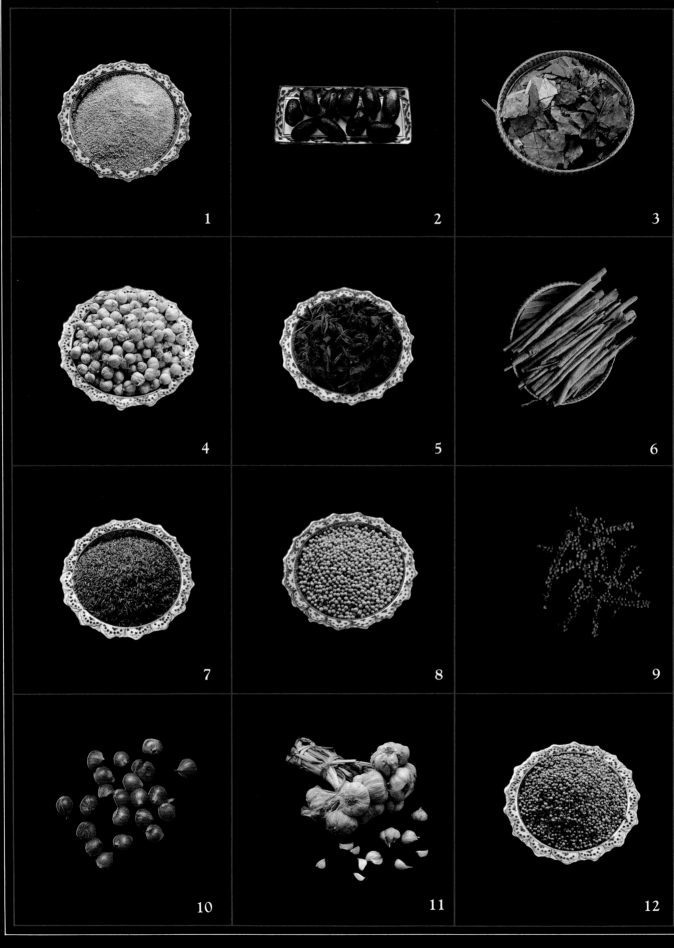

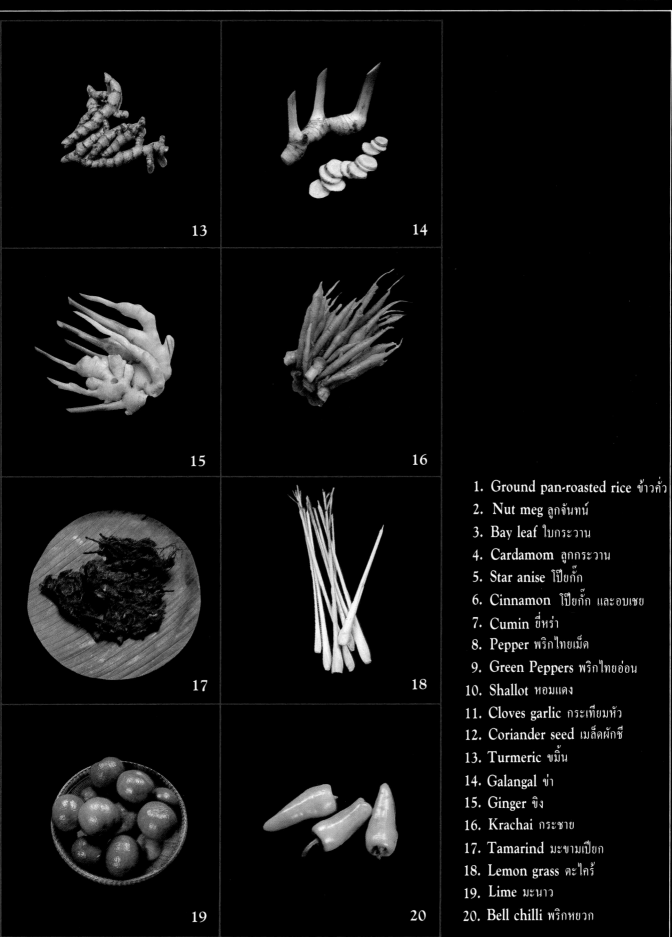

1. Ground pan-roasted rice ข้าวคั่ว
2. Nut meg ลูกจันทน์
3. Bay leaf ใบกระวาน
4. Cardamom ลูกกระวาน
5. Star anise โป๊ยกั๊ก
6. Cinnamon โป๊ยกั๊ก และอบเชย
7. Cumin ยี่หร่า
8. Pepper พริกไทยเม็ด
9. Green Peppers พริกไทยอ่อน
10. Shallot หอมแดง
11. Cloves garlic กระเทียมหัว
12. Coriander seed เมล็ดผักชี
13. Turmeric ขมิ้น
14. Galangal ข่า
15. Ginger ขิง
16. Krachai กระชาย
17. Tamarind มะขามเปียก
18. Lemon grass ตะไคร้
19. Lime มะนาว
20. Bell chilli พริกหยวก

Tapioca flour, paeng man sampalang, แป้งมันสำปะหลัง, is made from tapioca, or cassava, tubers. When this or any of the other flour is used to thicken a sauce, it is first mixed well with a little water so that it will not lump in the sauce.

NOODLES

Rice noodles, kuai-tiao, เส้นก๋วยเตี๋ยว, are flat white noodles made from rice flour and are cut into strips of three widths: **wide** (2-3 cm), sen yai, เส้นใหญ่, **narrow** (about 5 mm), sen lek, เส้นเล็ก, and **thin** (1-2 mm), sen mi, เส้นหมี่. Uncut fresh noodles sheets are sold in the market, as are fresh wide and narrow rice noodles. Thin noodles are available dried, and wide and narrow noodles may also be bought in this form. Dried noodles are soaked in water before use to soften them.

Vermicelli, khanom jin, ขนมจีน, are thin, round noodles, also made from rice flour, and sold fresh in the form of wads that look like birds' nests. They should be eaten within a few days of being made, and it is a good practice to steam them after bringing them home from the market.

Egg noodles, ba mi, บะหมี่, are yellow noodles made from wheat flour. Small balls of this kind of noodles are available in the market.

Mungbean noodles, wun sen, วุ้นเส้น, are thread-like noodles made from mung bean flour. They are sold dried and are soaked in water before use. When cooked, they become transparent. High quality noodles maintain their integrity in soup better than do cheap ones.

SUGARS

Sugar, nam tan sai, น้ำตาลทราย, is granulated cane sugar. Colors range from white to reddish and textures from fine to coarse. Some people find the reddish sugar tastier than the more highly refined white. The cleanliness of sugars in the market varies so it is wise to inspect carefully for foreign matter before purchase. Even so, some debris, such as tiny threads of cane, may remain and thus the recipes call for the straining of sugar solutions when clarity is desired.

Palm sugar, nam tan pip, น้ำตาลปีบ, was originally made from the sap of the sugar, or palmyra, palm, *Borassus flabellifera,* called tan in Thai, which has a very rough trunk and large, fan-shaped leaves. Now it is generally made from the sap of coconut palms, and may be sold as coconut sugar. The sugar is a light goldenbrown paste with a distinctive flavor and fragrance. It is put up in five-gallon kerosene cans, called pip in Thai.

FISH AND MEAT

Fish sauce, nam pla, น้ำปลา, is a clear, brown liquid derived from a brew of fish or shrimp mixed with salt. It is sold in bottles and plastic jugs as well as in earthenware jars. High quality fish sauce has a fine aroma and taste. Fish sauce is placed on the table as a condiment at nearly every meal, either as is or mixed with sliced chillies and perhaps lime juice.

Oyster sauce, nam man hoi, น้ำมันหอย, is a sweetened soy sauce to which oyster extract is added.

Salted fish, pla khem, ปลาเค็ม, is dried, salted sea fish, such as pla insee, ปลาอินทรี. In the market, the seller will cut you a steak of the required thickness. This is slowly roasted for a time to bring out the aroma.

Dried fish, pla haeng, ปลาแห้ง, is a fresh-water fish, such as serpent head, which is slit open, gutted, and spread to dry in the sun.

Shrimp paste, ka-pi, กะปิ, is shrimp which are salted, perhaps brewed for a time, allowed to dry in the sun, then ground into a fine-textured puce paste, which is fragrant and slightly salty.

Dried shrimp, kung haeng, กุ้งแห้ง, are small shrimp which have been dried in the sun. The quality product is plump orange and whitish shrimp with a minimum of debris.

Mackerel, pla thu, ปลาทู, is a small saltwater fish, *Rastrelliger chrysozonus* (Scombridae). Steamed mackerel in small woven trays are sold in food shops nearly everywhere in the country; **fresh mackerel,** pla thu sot, ปลาทูสด, are available at the fish-monger's in the market.

Sea perch, pla kaphong, ปลากะพง, is a general name for fish of the sea bass and sea perch families.

Rock cod, pla kao, ปลาเก๋า, is also known as grouper, reef cod, and sea bass.

Serpent head, pla chon, ปลาช่อน, is the freshwater fish *Ophiocephalus striatus.*

Featherback, pla krai, ปลากราย, is the freshwater fish *Notopterus chitala.*

Pork belly, mu sam chan, หมูสามชั้น, is bacon-cut pork, with layers of red meat, fat and skin.

Pig Skin, nang mu, หนังหมู, is used in many Thai dishes. It is boiled for use in spicy salads and also deep fried. Before use, all hair and fat must be removed and the skin must be scraped. It is then boiled until tender and then sliced. The skin from the belly is preferred because it is more tender than that from the back.

Chicken stock, nam sup, น้ำซุป, made from chicken is preferred in Thai cooking. While plain water can substitute and while the instant chicken broth cubes and pastes marketed by various food manufacturers are certainly fast and convenient. It might be interesting to make up this stock: Chop 3.5 lbs. chicken bones and scrap into 3-4 inch long pieces, place in a pot with 10 cups water and allow to stand 30 minutes. Peel 1 Chinese radishes, cut in half lengthwise and add to pot. Wash 3 celery plants and 3 garlic plants, remove the roots, coil the plants together, tie into a bundle, and add to pot, together with 5 bay leaves and 1 tbsp. salt. Heat to boiling, simmer over low heat for 1-1½ hours, and then strain through cheesecloth.

BEANS AND BEAN PRODUCTS

Beancurd, tao hu, เต้าหู้, is made up salted and unsalted in solid and soft forms. The solid curd has a cheesy consistency and is sold in blocks about four inches square. The blocks of the unsalted curd are white while those of the salted, **yellow beancurd,** tao hu leuang, เต้าหู้เหลือง, are yellow on the outside and off-white inside. The solid curd is used in fried dishes. The **soft white beancurd,** tao hu khao chanit on, เต้าหู้ขาวชนิดอ่อน, is cut into bricks for sale and is used in soups.

Fermented soybeans, tao jiao, เต้าเจี้ยว, is a brew of soybeans and salt.

Soybean paste, tao jiao nam, เต้าเจี้ยวน้ำ, is a preparation made with fermented soybeans and flour.

Soy sauces, si-iu, ซีอิ๊ว, used in these recipes are of the Chinese, rather than the Japanese, type.

Light soy sauce, si-iu khao, ซีอิ๊วขาว, is a clear brown liquid used in much the same way that fish sauce is.

Dark soy sauce, si-iu dam, ซีอิ๊วดำ, is opaque, black, viscous, and sweet. It is mixture of soy sauce and molasses.

Black beans, thua dam, ถั่วดำ, are a small dark bean sold dry and used in sweets.

Mungbeans, thua khiao, ถั่วเขียว, are yellow beans with green shells. The shelled bean is used in sweets and the whole bean is sprouted, giving, **bean sprouts,** thua ngok, ถั่วงอก.

HERBS AND SPICES

Ginger, khing, ขิง, *Zingiber officinale,* grows from an underground stem, or rhisome. Mature ginger stems are buff colored; **young or fresh ginger,** khing on, ขิงอ่อน, is white and is eaten fresh and pickled as well as cooked.

Galangal, kha, ข่า, *Alpinia galangal,* is a largar and lighter-colored relative of ginger and has its own distinctive taste.

Krachai, กระชาย, *Kaempferia panduratum,* grows bunches of slender and short yellow-brown tuberous roots and is used in fish dishes.

Turmeric, kha-min, ขมิ้น, *Curcuma longa,* is a small ginger with brown rhisomes. Inside, the flesh is a bright carrot orange. An important use is as a coloring agent.

Lemon grass, ta-khrai, ตะไคร้, *Cymbopgon citratus,* is an aromatic grey-green grass. The bases of the stems are used in cookery.

Shallot, hom lek, หอมเล็ก, or hom daeng, หอมแดง, *Allium ascalonicum,* is the zesty small red onion favored in Thai cooking.

Onion, hom hua yai, หอมหัวใหญ่, *Allium cepa,* has light colored bulbs that are larger and milder that those of the shallot.

Cinnamon, op-choey, อบเชย, *Cinnamomum spp.,* is the bark of a number of species of trees in this

21

22

23

24

25

26

21. **Small dried chillies** พริกแห้งเล็ก
    Big dried chillies พริกแห้งใหญ่
    Ground dried chillies พริกป่น
22. **Hot chillies** พริกขี้หนู
23. **Red and Yellow spur chillies**
    พริกชี้ฟ้าแดงและพริกชี้ฟ้าเหลือง
24. **Kaffir-lime** ลูกมะกรูด
    Kaffir lime leaves ใบมะกรูด
25. **Onion** หอมหัวใหญ่
26. **Spring onion** ต้นหอม
27. **Chinese chives** ต้นกุยช่าย
28. **Celery** ใบขึ้นฉ่าย
29. **Sweet basil** (maeng lak) ใบแมงลัก
30. **Sweet basil** (horopha) ใบโหระพา
31. **Mint** สะระแหน่
32. **Basil** (Kraproa) ใบกะเพรา
33. **Garlic plant** ต้นกระเทียม
34. **Coriander green** ผักชี

genus, classified in the laurel family. The types that grow in Southeast Asia are known in commerce as cassias. The barks, which are generally reddish-brown, after being peeled off from around the branch, tend to roll themselves back up, and so have a scroll-like appearance. For retail sale in Thai markets, the bark is cut into stirps about 1 cm across

Garlic, kra-thiam, กระเทียม. Thai garlic has small cloves covered with a peel that is not tough. Its fragrance is stronger than that of large-cloved garlic. In making fried garlic, the peel is usually not removed entirely so that only the flesh remains. Some of the peel is left on the clove, for it is in the peel that the fragrance resides.

Garlic is an ingredient in all types of curries as well as of stir-fried and deep-fried dishes. The fragrance of garlic is one hallmark of Thai cooking.

Garlic is also used raw. Thin slices are mixed with chilli and fish sauce and used as a garnish by those who like their food hot.

In addition to fresh garlic, Thai cooking utilizes **pickled garlic,** kra-thiam dong กระเทียมดอง. Mature, freshly harvested garlic is pickled in a brine made up from vinegar, sugar, and salt. It is used in making dishes and also served with curries.

The type of garlic which is preferred for pickling with honey has bulbs with just one clove. These garlic rounds are not a separate variety of garlic but a natural phenomenon whereby a **garlic bulb** kra-thiam thon กระเทียมโทน does not divide into many cloves. In the sorting of pickled garlic, 20 to 30 kilograms yields only 1 to 2 kilograms of garlic rounds, and therefore, they are expensive.

Garlic lends a characteristic fragrance to Thai food and, in addition to this, a spicy taste. This aroma helps mask unpleasant odors of other ingredients.

Star anise, poi-kak, โป๊ยกั๊ก, has a delicate aroma and is used both whole and ground. Before use, it must be roasted to bring out the aroma.

Chillies, phrik, พริก, *Capsicum annuum,* of several varieties are available in Thailand. As they ripen, they change color from green to red and become hotter. Fully ripe fruits are dried in the sun to give **dried chillies,** phrik haeng, พริกแห้ง, and these are pounded for **ground dried chilli,** phrik pon, พริกป่น.

Hot chillies, phrik khi nu, พริกขี้หนู, are the hottest type and also the smallest, being only about a centimeter long.

Green pepper, phrik-thai-awn, พริกไทยอ่อน, is almost mature pepper berries which are pruned from the vines in thinning so that the remaining berries can develop fully. When nearly ripe pepper corns are dried in the sun, they are called black pepper, and when fully matured corns are sun dried, they take on a whitish color, and so are called white pepper. Black pepper is not so hot as white pepper, and so green pepper is not very hot.

Green pepper is used in curries made without coconut milk, in Thai-style stir-fried dishes, and in chilli sauces. If kept long, green pepper will go bad, so it is usually not washed. If it is washed, it should be dried and then placed in a container in the refrigerator. Green pepper is not as fragrant as dried pepper.

Bell chilli, phrik yuak, พริกหยวก, is light green in color and mild in taste. They are used in spicy salads and chilli pastes for their fragrance, and in stir-fried meat dishes for both flavor and aroma.

Dried chilli, phrik haeng, พริกแห้ง, is fully ripened, red spur chillies dried either in the sun or by smoking. They may be large or small, depending on the variety of spur chilli used. They are prepared by removing the seeds, soaking in water, and then pounding in a mortar. Bright red dried chillies should be selected for the color they lend chilli pastes. Smoked chillies are darker in color.

Ground Chilli, phrik pon, พริกป่น. There are two types of ground chilli: ground spur chilli and ground hot chilli, the former being less hot than the latter. Both are dried and pan roasted before being ground, and are put up for sale in plastic bag. It is best to buy small quantities because, if kept long, the aroma is lost. Dried chilli is used in spicy chopped meat salads, spicy salads, sour and spicy soups, and in sauces. It is also a table condiment, used by Thais in the way Westerners use pepper.

Nutmeg and Mace, luk jan and dawk jan, ลูกจันทน์ และดอกจันทน์ Nutmeg is a dark brown, egg-shaped seed and mace is the yellowish-brown, petal-like covering of the seed.

Nutmeg is roasted before use to bring out its fragrance and is employed in chilli pastes and boiled meat dishes. In traditional Thai boiled beef, nutmeg is added to mask the odor of the meat. Ground nutmeg loses its aroma quickly, so Thai cooks buy nutmeg seeds and roast and grind them as required.

Mace sections are sword shaped and are used, roasted and ground, in Indian-style curries, Northern-style chopped meat salad, boiled beef, sateh sauce, and Tavoy-style spicy salad.

Mint leaves, sa-ra-nae, สะระแหน่. Thai mint leaves are round, not thick, hairless, and slightly wavy. The stem tends to be dark red. It is easy to grow, and Thais commonly plant it in pots kept near the kitchen, where it can always be easily gathered.

Mint leaves are deep green and fragrant, especially after being washed and chopped. They have a slightly hot taste. They are served fresh with spicy salads and as an ingredient in spicy chopped meat salads, spicy salads, and in sour and spicy fish soups.

For foods like spicy meat salads, mint leaves are a must.

Holy Basil, ka-phrao, กะเพรา. There are two types of holy basil, light and dark, the latter being dark purple. The dark type is fragrant when heated. Holy basil is also eaten fresh. Light holy basil is not used much except in spicy salads because they are not so fragrant. With a slightly hot flavor, though not so hot as pepper, holy basil leaves are used in many Thai dishes, including stir-fried meat dishes and curries.

Holy basil is easily grown in Thailand. The stems break easily, so in picking, stems are broken from the plant, and soon new stems sprout. Also, the seeds fall and new plants spring up.

Sweet basil, maenglak, แมงลัก, is a bright light green plant with a tangy taste.

Sweet basil, horapha, โหระพา, is an attractive plant with deep green leaves and often reddish stems. It has a taste reminiscent of anise.

Cloves, kan phlu, กานพลู, are the very fragrant tack-like flower buds of the tree *Caryophyllus aromaticus,* thought to be native to insular Southeast Asia.

Cumin, yi-ra, ยี่หร่า, *Cuminium cyminum,* has elongated yellow-brown seeds about 5 mm in length, which are ridged longitudinally and often have a seed stalk attached. They are roasted before use to heighten their fragrance.

Sesame, nga, งา, *Sesamum indium,* has small oval seeds which are white and have dark hulls. They are usually sold hulled.

Cardamoms, luk kra-wan, ลูกกระวาน, *Amomum krevanh,* appear like miniature unhusked coconuts. The off-white, bulbshaped capsules reach about 1 cm in length and slightly more than this in diameter. Inside is a densely-packed cluster of angular, dark brown seeds, which are aromatic and have a slightly hot taste.

Bay leaf, bai kra-wan, ใบกระวาน, is an elliptical leaf about 7 cm long, greygreen on the bottom, having a brownish cast on the top, which is sold dried in the market.

Coriander, phak chi, ผักชี, *Coriandrum sativum,* is of the parsley family. The leaves and stems are eaten fresh and used frequently as a garnish. The root and the seeds are ingredients in many dishes. The root is taken from the fresh plant. The seeds which are roughly spherical, 2-4 cm in diameter, and range in color from off-white to brown, have a pleasant taste and fragrance. They can be bought in the market. It is better to roast and grind seeds immediately before use than to buy ground coriander seed.

Pepper, phrik thai, พริกไทย, *Piper nigrum,* produces berries, which, when ripe, are dried and ground with the skins on to give black pepper, or with the skins off to give white pepper. The most widely available form in Thailand is white pepper.

Pandanus leaf, bai toey, ใบเตย, *Pandanus odorus,* the long, bright green leaf of a small palm and is used in making sweets.

FRUITS AND VEGETABLES

Eggplant, ma-kheua, มะเขือ, *Solanum spp,* are eaten with nam phrik. There are a number of types, ranging in size from that of a ping-pong ball down to that of a marble, in shape from that of an egg to that of a flattened sphere, and in color from green and white to yellow. One small type is called **me-kheua pro,** มะเขือเปราะ.

Ma-kheua phuang, มะเขือพวง, *Solanum torvum,* grow in clusters and, when yet unripe, look like large peas.

35

36

37

38

39

40

41

42

43

35. Yard-long bean ถั่วฝักยาว
36. Kale ผักคะน้า
37. Baby corns ข้าวโพดอ่อน
38. Bean sprout ถั่วงอก
39. Wing bean ถั่วพลู
40. Coconut มะพร้าว
41. Cucumber แตงกวา
42. Lettuce ผักกาดหอม
43. Swamp cabbage ผักบุ้ง
44. Ma-Kheua phuang มะเขือพวง
    Ma-Kheua pro มะเขือเปราะ
45. Sponge gourd บวบเหลี่ยม
46. Wax gourd ฟัก
47. Cabbage กะหล่ำปลี
48. Banana blossom หัวปลี

Long eggplant, ma-kheua yao, มะเขือยาว, has a long green fruit.

Yard-long beans, thua fak yao, ถั่วฝักยาว, have pods up to 60 cm long. These are eaten both fresh and cooked and are at their best when young and slender.

Winged bean, thua phu, ถั่วพู, bears a pod which in cross section looks like a rectangle that has a fringe-like extension at each corner, the "wings" of the bean.

Banana, Nam Wa variety, kluai nam wa, กล้วยน้ำว้า, *Musa sapientum,* probably the most popular eating banana among the nearly thirty varieties found in Thailand, has short oblong fruits that become a pale yellow as they ripen. The leaf, bai tong, ใบตอง, of this variety is used in Pla Kao Rat Sot Ma-kheua Thet in Banana Leaf. Wrapping goes more easily if the sections are torn and allowed to stand overnight before wrapping.

Coconut, ma-phrao, มะพร้าว, *Cocos nucifera,* is found nearly everywhere people have settled in all parts of the country and its production is important to the economy. The use to coconut milk in curries is a hallmark of Thai cooking. The meat of ripe nuts is scraped either by hand or by machine. The grated coconut is placed in a basin and mixed with a certain amount of warm water. The coconut is then picked up in the hand, held over a second container, and squeezed to press out the **coconut milk,** ka-thi, กะทิ. A finemeshed strainer should be positioned below the hand during squeezing to catch any meat that falls. Many cooks add a little salt to the water or the milk.

Coconut cream, hua ka-thi, หัวกะทิ, can be obtained by mixing a little warm water with the grated coconut and collecting the required amount of cream on the first squeezing. Following this, water can be added again and the grated coconut can be squeezed a second and a third time to obtain a less rich milk, which is kept separate from the cream. Alternatively, the full amount of warm water may be mixed with the grated coconut. After squeezing, the liquid is allowed to stand for a time, and then the cream is skimmed from top with a spoon.

Fastidious cooks scrape mature brown coconuts themselves by hand and coconut thus grated is usually pure white. In the market, however, the work is done with a machine that accepts chunks of coconut cut from the shell and usually a thin layer of shell still adheres to the meat. As a result, the grated coconut sold in the market is flecked with tiny brown particles of shell. This is useable for making coconut milk but is unacceptable when the grated coconut itself is to be used, for example, as a topping for a sweet. For such purposes, the recipes specify **white grated coconut,** ma-phrao khao, มะพร้าวขาว, which is also available in the market.

For the sake of efficiency in extracting coconut milk, grated coconut is quite fine, but in making sweets, a coarser cut is sometimes desired. This **shredded coconut,** ma-phrao theun theuk khut kratai jin, มะพร้าวทึนทึกขูดกระต่ายจีน, is sold in the market and is obtained by using a special scraper. This lacking, the top of a soft drink bottle might be used to scrape threads of coconut meat.

For those who wish to avoid the bother of scraping and squeezing, ready-made coconut milk is offered by food processors. This can be used in the recipes simply by measuring out the amount specified. In recipes which distinguish coconut cream from coconut milk, coconut cream is approximated by the ready-made coconut milk used full strength right from the container, while coconut milk may be approximated by mixing one part of the ready-made product with one part water.

Lime, ma-nao, มะนาว, *Citrus acida,* has small spherical fruits which are green or yellow. Lemon may be used.

Kaffir lime, ma-krut, มะกรูด, Citrus hystrix, has green fruits with wrinkled skin. The rind and the leaves are used in cookery.

Tamarind, ma-kham, มะขาม, *Tamarindus indica,* is a tree which bears tan pods inside of which are bean-like hard brown seeds surrounded by sticky flesh. The tan pod shell can be removed easily. **Ripe tamarind,** ma-kham piak, มะขามเปียก, is the flesh, seeds, and veins, of several fruit pressed together in the hand to form a wad.

Tamarind juice, nam som ma-kham, น้ำส้มมะขาม, is obtained by mixing some of the ripe fruit with water and squeezing out the juice. The immature fruit and the young leaves and flowers are also used, all to give a sour taste. There are also sweet tamarinds which are a delight to eat and command a high price.

Mushrooms, het, เห็ด, of many types are available fresh. The most common is the **rice straw mushroom,** het fang, เห็ดฟาง.

Ear mushroom, het hu nu, เห็ดหูหนู, is a dark greyish brown fungus that has a delightful crunchy texture.

Shiitake mushroom, het hom, เห็ดหอม, is available dried in the market.

Spring onion, ton hom, ต้นหอม, *Allium fistulosum,* also called green onion or scallion, has leaves that are circular in cross section. These are much used as a garnish. The bases of the plant are frequently served on the side of one-dish meals, such as fried rice, or placed on the salad plate.

Garlic plant, ton kra-thiam, ต้นกระเทียม, *Allium sativum,* is the young plant picked before the bulb has formed. The leaves are flat and folded length-wise.

Chinese chives, ton kui chai, ต้นกุยช่าย, *Allium tuberosum,* has fairly thick, narrow, flat leaves which are eaten with fried noodle dishes such as Phat Thai.

Celery, kheun chai, ขึ้นฉ่าย, *Apium graveolens,* also called celeriae, turniprooted celery, or Chinese soup celery, has very small stalks (only a few millimeters across) and a very strong flavor.

Chinese radish, hua phak kat, หัวผักกาด, or hua chai thao, หัวไชเท้า, *Raphanus sativus* (longpinnatus variety), has a long, cylindrical root that looks like a hefty white carrot.

Chinese cabbage, phak kat khao, ผักกาดขาว, *Brassica campestris* (pekinensis variety), has thin, light green leaves and broad, flat, and thin leaf ribs which form an elongated, rather than a spherical, head.

Kale, phak kha-na, ผักคะน้า, *Brassica oleracea* (acephala variety), has leathery grey-green leaves on thick stalks. Stalk lovers buy the large variety, while those partial to the leaves get the dwarf variety.

Chinese mustard green, phak kwang tung, ผักกวางตุ้ง, *Brassica campestris* (chinensis variety), has dark green oval leaves on thick fleshy stalks.

Swamp cabbage, phak bung, ผักบุ้ง, *Ipomoea aquatica,* also called water convolvulus, water spinach, or aquatic morning glory, has hollow stems and roughly triangular leaves. The Thai variety has delicate dark green leaves and deep red stalks while the Chinese is thicker, larger, and lighter green. The tender tips of the stems are eaten fresh or cooked.

Sponge gourd, buap liam, บวบเหลี่ยม, *Luffa acutangula,* also called vegetable gourd or Chinese okra, is oblong, pointed, and dark green and has sharp longitudinal ridges.

Wax gourd, fak khiao, ฟักเขียว, *Benincasa hispida,* also called white gourd or Chinese preserving melon, is oblong and light green to white. The ends are rounded and the flesh is solid and white.

Cucumber, taeng kwa, แตงกวา, *Cucumis sativus,* has short fruits about 8 cm long which are crispiest while still green and white, before yellowing. A larger type, taeng ran, แตงร้าน, are also eaten.

Water chestnut, haeo, แห้ว, is the tuber of certain kinds of sedges. The skin is dark and the crunchy meat inside is off-white.

Tomatoes, ma-kheua thet, มะเขือเทศ, of three types are used in Thai cooking. The first is small, round fruits, not much bigger than a pea, which grow in clusters and have a sweet and sour taste. These are used in Northern and Northeastern dishes.

Large-sized tomatoes are sweet and are used in sour and spicy soups and in spicy salads.

The third type is **cherry tomatoes.** These have a sweet and sour taste and are used in Northeastern-style papaya salad as well as in curries and sour and spicy soups.

Bady corn, khao phot awn, ข้าวโพดอ่อน, is harvested from special varieties of corn before the ear has matured. It is stir-fried with pork, boiled and eaten with chilli pastes, and served fresh with coconut sauce.

Pickled plum, buai dong, บ๊วยดอง, is the preserved fruit of an oriental plum which is sometimes labeled Japanese apricot.

PREPARED SPICE MIXTURES

Five spice powder, phong pha-loh, ผงพะโล้, is a prepared mixture of spices, among which is star anise, poi-kak, โป๊ยกั๊ก, *Ilicium verum.*

Curry powder, phong ka-ri, ผงกะหรี่, is a prepared mixture of spices such as turmeric, coriander seed, ginger, cloves, cinnamon, mustard, cardamom, cumin, chilli, and salt. Each brand has its own character depending on the ingredients used.

Table of Contents

Soup and Steamed Dishes

Curry Dishes

Spicy Salad Dishes

107. SALAT KHAEK
(Southern Thai Salad)
สลัดแขก

109. YAM WUN SEN
(Spicy Mungbean Noodle Salad)
ยำวุ้นเส้น

111. YAM PLA KRAPONG
(Spicy Sardine Salad)
ยำปลากระป๋อง

YAM KHAI TOM
(Spicy Egg Salad)
ยำไข่ต้ม

113. YAM SAIKROK KAP HAEM
(Spicy Frankfurter-and-Ham Salad)
ยำไส้กรอกกับแฮม

115. YAM KAI YANG
(Spicy Barbecued-Chicken Salad)
ยำไก่ย่าง

117. LAP KAI
(Savory Chopped-Chicken Salad)
ลาบไก่

119. LAP MU
(Savory Pork Chopped Salad)
ลาบหมู

121. PHLA MU OP
(Savory Baked Pork Salad)
พล่าหมูอบ

123. YAM PLA MEUK
(Spicy Squid Salad)
ยำปลาหมึก

125. PHLA KUNG
(Savory Prawn Salad)
พล่ากุ้ง

127. NEUA NAM TOK
(Savory Beef Salad)
เนื้อน้ำตก

Other Main Dishes

129. KUNG PHAO
(Charcoal-Broiled large prawns with Savory Sauce)
กุ้งเผา

131. KAI KOLAE
(Southern-Thai-Style Braised Chicken)
ไก่กอและ

133. PET THOT SOT SAI
(Baked Stuffed Duck)
เป็ดทอดสอดไส้

135. KAI OP NAM DAENG
(Braised Chicken)
ไก่อบน้ำแดง

137. PET OP KROP
(Crispy Baked Duck)
เป็ดอบกรอบ

139. KAI YANG
(Thai-Style Barbecued Chicken)
ไก่ย่าง

141. KHUNG YANG SOT MAKHAM PIAK
(Broiled Lobsters in Tamarind Sauce)
กุ้งย่างซอสมะขามเปียก

143. SI-KHRONG MU YANG
(Barbecued Spareribs)
ซี่โครงหมูย่าง

145. KHA MU TOM PHALO
(Boiled Fresh Ham with the Five Spices)
ขาหมูต้มพะโล้

147. PLA KAO OP SOT MA-KHEUA THET
(Baked Rock Cod in Tomato Sauce)
ปลาเก๋าอบซอสมะเขือเทศ

149. PHA O YANG SI IU
(Broiled Tunny with Soy Sauce)
ปลาโอย่างซีอิ๊ว

151. LON HAEM
(Coconut Ham Sauce)
หลนแฮม

153. NAM PHRIK ONG
(Pork and Tomato Chilli Dip)
น้ำพริกอ่อง

One-Plate Dishes

Sweets

CURRY PASTES

NAM PHRIK KAENG DAENG
(Red Curry Paste)

INGREDIENTS:

13 small dried chillies, soaked in hot water for 15 minutes and deseeded
3 tbsp. chopped shallot
4 tbsp. chopped garlic
1 tbsp. chopped galangal
2 tbsp. chopped lemon grass
2 tsp. chopped kaffir lime rind
1 tbsp. chopped coriander root
20 pepper corns
1 tsp. shrimp paste
1 tbsp. coriander seed
1 tsp. cumin seed

PREPARATION:

1. In a wok over low heat, put the coriander seeds and cumin seeds and dry fry for about 5 minutes, then grind into a powder.

2. Into a blender, put the rest of the ingredients except the shrimp paste and blend to mix well. The add the coriander seed-cumin seed mixture and the shrimp paste and blend again to obtain about 3/4 cup of a fine-textured paste.

3. This can be stored in a glass jar in the refrigerator for about 3-4 months.

NAM PHRIK KAENG KHUA
(Kaeng Khua Curry Paste)

INGREDIENTS:

5 dried chillies, soaked in hot water for 15 minutes and deseeded
3 tbsp. chopped shallots
2 tbsp. chopped garlic
1 tsp. chopped galangal
1 tbsp. chopped lemon grass
1 tsp. chopped kaffir lime rind
1 tsp. chopped coriander root
2 tsp. salt
1 tsp. shrimp paste

PREPARATION:

1. Into a blender, put all ingredients except the shrimp paste and blend until well mixed. Then, add the shrimp paste and blend once more to obtain about 3/4 cup of a fine-textured paste.

2. This can be stored in a glass jar in the refrigerator for about 3-4 months.

NAM PHRIK PHAO
(Roasted Chili Sauce)

INGREDIENTS:

1/2 cup small dried chillies
3 tbsp. fish sauce
2 cups vegetable oil
1/3 tsp. salt
8 shallots, sliced
6 garlic cloves, sliced
1 cup dried shrimp
1 tbsp. palm sugar
1 1/2 tbsp. tamarind juice

PREPARATION:

1. Heat the oil in a wok and fry the shallots and garlic until golden brown; remove from oil and drain. Add the dried shrimp and dried chillies; fry until golden brown; remove from oil and drain.

2. In a mortar or blender, grind the shrimp, garlic, chillies, shallots and sugar until the mixture is blended well. Add the fish sauce, tamarind juice, salt and cooled oil from the wok into the blender; blend until you have a finely textured sauce.

3. This can be stored in a glass jar in the refrigerator for about 3-4 months.

NAM PHRIK KAENG KHIAO WAN
(Green Curry Paste)

INGREDIENTS:

15 green hot chillies
3 tbsp. chopped shallots
1 tbsp. chopped garlic
1 tsp. chopped galangal
1 tbsp. chopped lemon grass
1/2 tsp. chopped kaffir lime rind
1 tsp. chopped coriander root
5 pepper corns
1 tbsp. coriander seeds
1 tsp. cumin seeds
1 tsp. salt
1 tsp. shrimp paste

PREPARATION:

1. In a wok over low heat, put the coriander seeds, and cumin seeds and dry fry for about 5 minutes, then grind into a powder.

2. Into a blender, put the rest of the ingredients except the shrimp paste and blend to mix well. Add the coriander-cumin seed mixture and the shrimp paste and blend to obtain 1/2 cup of a fine-textured paste.

3. This can be stored in a glass jar in the refrigerator for about 3-4 months.

NAM PHRIK KEANG KA-RI
(Yellow Curry Paste)

INGREDIENTS:

3 dried chillies, soaked in hot water for 15 minutes and deseeded
3 tbsp. chopped shallots
1 tbsp. chopped garlic
1 tsp. chopped ginger
1 tbsp. coriander seeds
1 tsp. cumin seeds
1 tbsp. chopped lemon grass
1 tsp. shrimp paste
1 tsp. salt
2 tsp. curry powder

PREPARATION:

1. In a wok over low heat, put the shallots, garlic, ginger, coriander seeds and cumin seeds and dry fry for about 5 minutes, then grind into a powder.

2. Into a blender, put the rest of the ingredients and blend to mix well. Add the shallot-garlic-ginger-coriander seed-cumin seed mixture and blend again to obtain about 1/2 cup of a fine-textured paste.

3. This can be stored in a glass jar in the refrigerator for about 3-4 months.

NAM PHRIK KAENG MATSAMAN
(Massaman Curry Paste)

INGREDIENTS:

3 dried chillies, soaked in hot water for 15 minutes and deseeded
3 tbsp. chopped shallots
2 tbsp. chopped garlic
1 tsp. chopped galangal
1 1/4 tbsp. chopped lemon grass
2 cloves
1 tbsp. coriander seeds
1 tsp. cumin seeds
5 pepper corns
1 tsp. shrimp paste
1 tsp. salt

PREPARATION:

1. In a wok over low heat put the shallots, garlic, galangal, lemon grass, cloves, coriander seeds, cumin seeds and dry fry for about 5 minutes, then grind into a powder.

2. Into a blender, put the rest of the ingredients except the shrimp paste and blend to mix well. Add the shallot-garlic-galangal-lemon grass-clove-coriander seed-cumin seed mixture and the shrimp paste and blend again to obtain 1/2 cup of a fine-textured paste.

3. This can be stored in a glass jar in the refrigerator for about 3-4 months.

KHAO TANG NA TANG
(Fried Potcrust and Dip)
ข้าวตังหน้าตั้ง

INGREDIENTS FOR FRIED POTCRUST :

300 grams rice-potcrust or bread
4 cups cooking oil

PREPARATION :

Place the oil in a deep wok over medium heat. When the oil is hot, fry the potcrust a few pieces at a time, turning as necessary until golden brown on both sides; then, remove from the oil and drain.
Bread can also be fried crisp in this way.

INGREDIENTS FOR DIP :

1/2 cup ground pork
1/2 cup ground prawn
1/4 cup ground roasted peanuts
1 3/4 cups coconut milk
1 dried chilli, seeds removed and soaked in water
1 tsp. sliced coriander root
1/4 tsp. pepper
4 cloves garlic
2 tbsp. sugar
1-2 tbsp. fish sauce
1 tbsp. thinly sliced shallot
1 coriander green, chopped

PREPARATION :

1. Pound the coriander root, pepper, chilli, and garlic well in a mortar.
2. Bring the coconut milk to a boil in a wok. When some oil has surfaced, add the coriander root, pepper, garlic mixture and stir to disperse. Next, add the prawn and pork, stir well and season to taste with the sugar and fish sauce. When the dip has come to a boil once again, add the peanut and shallot, remove from the heat, and sprinkle with a little chopped coriander greens.
3. Serve with fried potcrust, crisp fried bread, or melba toast. ·

5 Serving

เครื่องปรุงข้าวตัง

ข้าวตัง 300 กรัม
น้ำมันพืช 4 ถ้วย

วิธีทำ

ใส่น้ำมันลงในกระทะก้นลึก ตั้งไฟแรงปานกลางพอน้ำมันร้อน ใส่ข้าวตังลงทอดทีละน้อย กลับบ้างเพื่อให้เหลืองทั้งแผ่น แล้วตักขึ้นพักให้สะเด็ดน้ำมัน อาจทอดขนมปังให้กรอบใช้แทนข้าวตังได้

เครื่องปรุงหน้าตั้ง

หมูสับ 1/2 ถ้วย	กุ้งสับ 1/2 ถ้วย
ถั่วลิสงคั่วบด 1/4 ถ้วย	กะทิ 1 3/4 ถ้วย
พริกแห้งแกะเมล็ดออก แช่น้ำ 1 เม็ด	
รากผักชีหั่น 1 ช้อนชา	พริกไทย 1/4 ช้อนชา
กระเทียม 4 กลีบ	น้ำตาลทราย 2 ช้อนโต๊ะ
น้ำปลา 1-2 ช้อนโต๊ะ	หอมแดงซอย 1 ช้อนโต๊ะ
ผักชีหั่นหยาบ 1 ต้น	

วิธีทำ

1. โขลกรากผักชี พริกไทย พริกแห้ง กับกระเทียมให้ละเอียด
2. ใส่กะทิลงในกระทะตั้งไฟจนแตกมัน ใส่รากผักชี พริกไทย พริกแห้งกับกระเทียม คนให้กระจายเข้ากันแล้วใส่เนื้อหมู กุ้ง ลงไปคนอีกครั้ง ปรุงรสด้วยน้ำตาล น้ำปลา เมื่อส่วนผสมเดือดอีกครั้ง ใส่ถั่วและหัวหอม แล้วยกลงโรยผักชี เสิร์ฟกับข้าวตังทอด

KHANOM PANG NA KUNG ROI NGA
(Fried Canapés with Prawn Spread)
ขนมปังหน้ากุ้งโรยงา

INGREDIENTS :

8 slices bread
300 grams prawns
100 grams lean pork
1 egg
1 tsp. thinly sliced coriander root
5 cloves garlic
1/4 tsp. pepper
2 tsp. light soy sauce
1/4 tsp. salt
2 tbsp. white sesame seeds
3 cups cooking oil

PREPARATION :

1. Dry the bread in a low oven. Alternatively, use bread which has dried out, for this will absorb less oil and give you very crisp canapés.

2. Shell and clean the prawns, add the pork, and mince.

3. Remove the skins of the garlic cloves, place in a mortar with the coriander root and pepper, and pound to a fine paste.

4. Knead the pounded garlic mixture together with the minced pork and prawn; then, add the egg, soy sauce, and salt; knead once again until uniform in consistency.

5. Divide the mixture into eight portions and spread one portion on each slice of bread. Smooth the surface of the spread and then sprinkle with about 1/2 tsp. sesame seeds.

6. Heat the oil in a wok. When it is hot, fry each slice of bread spread-side downward. When the spread has become golden brown, remove the bread from the oil and drain on absorbent paper.

7. Cut each slice of bread into quarters, arrange on a serving platter, and serve with marmalade sauce or seasoning sauce and with fresh vegetables, such as chilled cucumber discs, or with pickles, such as pickled ginger.

INGREDIENTS FOR MARMALADE SAUCE :

1/4 cup marmalade
1/4 cup vinegar
1/4 tsp. salt

PREPARATION :

Mix the ingredients in a pot, heat with stirring just long enough to mix togerher well, and then transfer to a bowl.

4 Serving

เครื่องปรุง

ขนมปัง 8 แผ่น
กุ้ง 300 กรัม
หมูเนื้อสัน 100 กรัม
ไข่ไก่ 1 ฟอง
รากผักชีหั่นฝอย 1 ช้อนชา
กระเทียม 5 กลีบ พริกไทย 1/4 ช้อนชา
ซีอิ๊วขาว 2 ช้อนชา เกลือ 1/4 ช้อนชา
งาขาว 2 ช้อนโต๊ะ น้ำมันพืช 3 ถ้วย

วิธีทำ

๑. อบขนมปังในเตาอบไฟอ่อนให้ขนมปังแห้ง หรือใช้ขนมปังค้างคืนที่แห้ง เอง ขนมปังแห้ง ๆ จะไม่อมน้ำมันมากและกรอบดี

๒. โขลกรากผักชี กระเทียม พริกไทยให้ละเอียด

๓. สับกุ้งกับหมูเข้าด้วยกัน แล้วนวดกับรากผักชี กระเทียม พริกไทย ใส่ไข่ ใส่ซีอิ๊ว เกลือ นวดจนเป็นเนื้อเดียวกันทำเป็นหน้า

๔. แบ่งหน้าออกเป็น 8 ส่วน ทาบนขนมปัง 8 แผ่น โรยงาแล้วนำไป ทอดน้ำมันร้อนไฟไม่แรงโดยคว่ำหน้าลง เมื่อเหลืองดีแล้วตักขึ้นให้สะเด็ด น้ำมัน

๕. หั่นขนมปังเป็นแผ่นละ 4 ชิ้น จัดลงจานเสิร์ฟ เสิร์ฟกับน้ำจิ้มพร้อม ผักสดเช่น แตงกวากรอบ ๆ หรือผักดองเช่นขิงดอง

วิธีทำน้ำจิ้ม

ผสมแยมผิวส้ม 1/4 ถ้วย น้ำส้มสายชู 1/4 ถ้วย เกลือ 1/4 ช้อนชา คนจนเป็นเนื้อเดียวกันตั้งไฟพอเดือด ยกลง ตักใส่ถ้วย

KHANOM PANG NA MU
(Fried Canapés with Pork Spread)
ขนมปังหน้าหมู

INGREDIENTS :

10 slices bread
1 1/2 cups ground pork
1 beaten egg
1 tbsp. light soy sauce
2 tbsp. water
1 tsp. finely chopped coriander root
1/2 tsp. pepper
5 cloves garlic
1 coriander green
1 finely sliced red chilli
4 cups cooking oil

PREPARATION :

1. Blend the pork with half of the egg then add the soy sauce. Pound the coriander root, pepper, and garlic well in a mortar and then knead into the pork mixture, adding the water.

2. Cut the slices of bread into quarters; these may be either square or triangular. Dry the bread by heating in a low oven. Place about 1 tbsp. of the pork spread on each piece of bread and spread it so that it mound in the center and slopes smoothly right to the edges. Smear the spread with some of the remaining egg and decorate with coriander greens and slices of red chilli.

3. Heat the oil in a wok. When it is hot, fry the pieces of bread spread-side downward until golden brown; then, remove from the oil and drain.

4. Serve with slices of fresh cucumber or with cucumber relish (See p.157).

5-8 Serving

เครื่องปรุง

ขนมปัง 10 แผ่น
หมูสับหรือบด 1 1/2 ถ้วย
ไข่ไก่ ตีเข้ากัน 1 ฟอง
ซีอิ๊วขาว 1 ช้อนโต๊ะ น้ำ 2 ช้อนโต๊ะ
รากผักชีหั่นละเอียด 1 ช้อนชา
พริกไทย 1/2 ช้อนชา กระเทียม 5 กลีบ
ผักชี 1 ต้น พริกแดงหั่นฝอย 1 เม็ด
น้ำมันพืช 4 ถ้วย

วิธีทำ

1. คลุกเนื้อหมูกับไข่ครึ่งหนึ่งและซีอิ๊วขาว โขลกรากผักชี พริกไทย และกระเทียมให้ละเอียด ผสมกับเนื้อหมูเติมน้ำแล้วนวด

2. ตัดขนมปังออกเป็นแผ่นละ 4 ชิ้น เอาเข้าเตาอบ อบไฟอ่อนให้ขนมปังแห้งแล้วนำออกมาทาหน้าหมูสับ ชิ้นละประมาณ 1 ช้อนโต๊ะ ให้ขอบเรียบตรงกลางนูนทาหน้าด้วยไข่ที่เหลือ แต่งด้วยใบผักชีและพริกหั่นฝอย

3. ใส่น้ำมันลงกระทะลึกตั้งไฟพอน้ำมันร้อนไฟไม่แรง ทอดโดยใส่ขนมปังคว่ำหน้าลงจนเหลืองดี ตักขึ้นพักให้สะเด็ดน้ำมัน

4. เสิร์ฟกับแตงกวาสดหรืออาจาด (ดูหน้า157)

PO-PIA THOT
(Egg Rolls)
ปอเปี๊ยะทอด

INGREDIENTS :

500 grams pack egg-roll sheets
100 grams mungbean noodles
200 grams ground pork (or chicken)
100 grams crab meat
1 egg
1/2 cup shredded cabbage
1/2 cup shredded carrot
1/3 cup (5-6) dried ear mushrooms, chopped (soaked in hot water)
1/2 tbsp. black pepper
1 tbsp. light soy sauce
2 tsp. salt
1 tbsp. chopped garlic
3 cups cooking oil

Paste made by mixing 2 tbsp. wheat flour in 1/4 cup water and stirring over low heat.

PREPARATION :

1. Soak the noodles until soft, then cut into short lengths.
2. Mix pork, crab meat, egg, cabbage, carrot, mushroom, pepper, salt and light soy sauce together and then add the noodles and mix well.

3. Fry the garlic in 3 tbsp. oil and then add the pork-and-noodle mixture. Fry until fairly dry, then dip up and set aside to cool.
4. Place a tablespoonful of the filling on an egg roll sheet, fold the sheet over the filling, fold about half a turn, fold in the ends to close them; then, roll up tightly, sealing the sheet closed with the paste.
5. Deep fry in plenty of oil over low heat until crisp and golden brown.
6. Serve with sauce, sliced cucumber, and sweet basil leaves.

INGREDIENTS FOR EGG ROLL SAUCE :

1/4 cup vinegar
1/4 cup water
1/2 cup sugar
1 tsp. salt
1/2 tbsp. chilli, well pounded
1 tbsp. tapioca flour mixed in 2 tbsp. water

PREPARATION :

Mix the vinegar, water, sugar, salt and chilli, heat to boiling, add a little of the flour water, boil a short time, then remove from heat. Yield about 150 pieces.

6-8 Serving

เครื่องปรุง

แผ่นแป้งปอเปี๊ยะ 500 กรัม วุ้นเส้นห่อ 100 กรัม
เนื้อหมูหรือไก่สับหรือบด 200 กรัม
เนื้อปู 100 กรัม ไข่ไก่ 1 ฟอง
กะหล่ำปลีหั่นฝอย 1/2 ถ้วย แครอทหั่นฝอย 1/2 ถ้วย
เห็ดหูหนูแห้งแช่น้ำแล้วหั่นฝอย 1/3 ถ้วย
พริกไทย 1/2 ช้อนโต๊ะ ซีอิ๊วขาว 1 ช้อนโต๊ะ
เกลือ 2 ช้อนชา กระเทียมสับ 1 ช้อนโต๊ะ น้ำมันพืช 3 ถ้วย

แป้งเปียกทำจากแป้งสาลี 2 ช้อนโต๊ะ ผสมกับน้ำ 1/4 ถ้วย แล้วตั้งไฟอ่อน คนจนแป้งสุกใส

วิธีทำ

1. แช่วุ้นเส้นให้นุ่มแล้วตัดเป็นท่อนสั้น
2. ผสมเนื้อหมู เนื้อปู ไข่ กะหล่ำปลี แครอท เห็ด พริกไทย เกลือ ซีอิ๊ว เข้าด้วยกันแล้วใส่วุ้นเส้นเคล้าให้ทั่ว

3. เจียวกระเทียมในน้ำมัน 3 ช้อนโต๊ะ ใส่ส่วนผสมลงผัดให้แห้ง แล้ว ตักขึ้นพักไว้ให้เย็น ใช้เป็นไส้ปอเปี๊ยะ
4. ตักไส้ 1 ช้อนโต๊ะใส่ตรงกลางแผ่นแป้ง พับครึ่ง แล้วพับปลายซ้าย-ขวา เข้าหากัน แล้วม้วนตามยาวให้แน่น แล้วจึงทาตรงปลายด้วยแป้งเปียก บาง ๆ ม้วนให้สนิท
5. ทอดปอเปี๊ยะด้วยน้ำมันที่ร้อน ไฟไม่แรง ทอดจนเหลืองดีตักขึ้นพักให้ สะเด็ดน้ำมัน
6. จัดเสิร์ฟกับแตงกวาหั่นเป็นแว่น ๆ ใบโหระพาและน้ำจิ้ม

วิธีทำน้ำจิ้ม

ผสมน้ำส้มสายชู 1/4 ถ้วย น้ำ 1/4 ถ้วย น้ำตาลทราย 1/2 ถ้วย เกลือ 1/2 ช้อนชา พริกแดงโขลก 1/2 ช้อนโต๊ะ ตั้งไฟจนเดือด แล้วจึงเติมแป้งมัน 1 ช้อนชาละลายกับน้ำ 2 ช้อนโต๊ะ ทีละน้อยจนหมด ตั้งไฟจนเดือดสักครู่ ยกลง

MI KROP
(Crispy Fried Noodles)
หมี่กรอบ

INGREDIENTS :

150 grams thin rice noodles

1/4 cup finely chopped pork

1/4 cup finely chopped fresh shrimp

1 tbsp. chopped garlic and shallot

1 tbsp. fermented soybeans

1 tbsp. vinegar

1 tbsp. fish sauce

4 tbsp. palm sugar

1 tsp. ground dried chillies

1 tbsp. lime juice

1 cake yellow beancurd, cut into matchstick-size pieces and fried crisp

2 pickled garlic bulbs, thinly sliced

1 chilli, thinly sliced

3 Chinese chives (gao choy)

50 grams bean sprouts

3 cups cooking oil

1 tbsp. thinly sliced kaffir lime rind

PREPARATION :

1. If the noodles are very fine, fry in oil until crisp and golden, then drain. If the noodles are thick, soak 15 minutes in water, drain well, and then fry a few at a time.

2. Heat 1/4 cup oil in a frying pan. Fry the garlic and shallot until fragrant, then add the pork and shrimp, seasoning with fermented soybeans, vinegar, fish sauce, sugar, dried chillies. When thick, add the lime juice. Mix and season to obtain a sweet, sour, and salty flavor.

3. Reduce the heat, add the noodles and continue turning in the sauce until they stick together; then, add the beancurd; mix, and spoon onto plates.

4. Sprinkle with the pickled garlic, chilli, thinly sliced kaffir lime rind or add coriander leaves more. Place bean sprouts and Chinese chives on the sides of the plates.

4 Serving

เครื่องปรุง

เส้นหมี่ 150 กรัม

เนื้อหมูสับหรือบด 1/4 ถ้วย

เนื้อกุ้งสับหรือบด 1/4 ถ้วย

กระเทียมกับหอมแดงสับ 1 ช้อนโต๊ะ

เต้าเจี้ยว 1 ช้อนโต๊ะ น้ำส้มสายชู 1 ช้อนโต๊ะ

น้ำปลา 1 ช้อนโต๊ะ น้ำตาลปีบ 4 ช้อนโต๊ะ

พริกป่น 1 ช้อนชา น้ำมะนาว 1 ช้อนโต๊ะ

เต้าหู้เหลืองหั่นเป็นชิ้นยาว ๆ บาง ๆ ขนาดก้านไม้ขีด แล้วทอดกรอบ 1 แผ่น

กระเทียมดองซอย 2 หัว

พริกหั่นฝอย 1 เม็ด กุยช่าย 3 ต้น

ถั่วงอก 50 กรัม น้ำมันพืช 3 ถ้วย

ใบมะกรูดหั่นฝอย 1 ช้อนโต๊ะ

วิธีทำ

1. ถ้าใช้หมี่ชนิดเส้นเล็กมาก ให้ทอดจนเหลืองกรอบ แล้วพักให้สะเด็ดน้ำมัน ถ้าหมี่เส้นหนา ให้แช่น้ำก่อนราว 15 นาที พักให้สะเด็ดน้ำแล้วจึงค่อย ๆ ใส่ลงกระทะ ทอดครั้งละน้อย ๆ จนหมด

2. ใส่น้ำมัน 1/4 ถ้วยลงในกระทะ เจียวกระเทียมกับหัวหอมจนหอมแล้วใส่เนื้อหมูกับกุ้งลงผัด ปรุงรสด้วยเต้าเจี้ยว น้ำส้ม น้ำปลา น้ำตาล และพริกป่น ผัดจนแห้งจึงเติมน้ำมะนาว ชิมรสตามชอบ รสออกหวานนำ ตามด้วยเปรี้ยวและเค็ม

3. หรี่ไฟ ใส่เส้นลงผัด คลุกให้เข้ากันดี แล้วใส่เต้าหู้คลุกอีกครั้ง ตักใส่จาน

4. โรยกระเทียมดอง พริก ใบมะกรูดหั่นฝอย หรือจะโรยผักชีซอยเพิ่มก็ได้ เสิร์ฟกับถั่วงอกและกุยช่าย

MU PAN KON THOT
(Fried Pork Meatballs)
หมูปั้นก้อนทอด

INGREDIENTS :

2 cups ground pork
1/2 tsp. salt
1 tbsp. fish sauce
1/2 tsp. pepper
1 tbsp. well-pounded garlic
2 tsp. well pounded coriander root
2 tbsp. water
1 cup cooking oil

PREPARATION :

1. Mix the pork, salt, fish sauce, pepper, garlic, coriander root and water together.

2. Take portions of the mixture of about one tablespoon and form into meatballs.

3. Place the oil in a wok on medium heat. When the oil is hot, fry the meatballs until golden; then, remove and drain.

4. Serve with pineapple, tomato, and spring onions.

4 *Serving*

เครื่องปรุง

หมูสับ 2 ถ้วย
เกลือป่น 1/2 ช้อนชา
น้ำปลา 1 ช้อนโต๊ะ
พริกไทยป่น 1/2 ช้อนชา
กระเทียมโขลกละเอียด 1 ช้อนโต๊ะ
รากผักชีโขลกละเอียด 2 ช้อนชา
น้ำ 2 ช้อนโต๊ะ
น้ำมันพืช 1 ถ้วย

วิธีทำ

1. ผสมหมูสับ เกลือ น้ำปลา พริกไทย กระเทียม รากผักชีและน้ำเข้าด้วยกัน

2. ตักส่วนผสมมาทีละประมาณ 1 ช้อนโต๊ะ ปั้นเป็นก้อนกลม

3. ตั้งน้ำมันใช้ไฟปานกลาง เมื่อน้ำมันร้อนทอดหมูที่ปั้นเป็นก้อนแล้วจนสุกเหลือง ตักขึ้น ทิ้งให้สะเด็ดน้ำมัน

4. เสิร์ฟกับสับปะรด มะเขือเทศ และต้นหอม

PU JA
(Fried Crab)
ปูจ๋า

INGREDIENTS :

3 meaty crabs
1 cup ground pork
1/2 tbsp. minced coriander root
1 tsp. minced garlic
1/4 tsp. pepper
1 1/2 tbsp. light soy sauce
1/4 tsp. salt
2 eggs
3 tbsp. fine breadcrumbs
2 cups cooking oil
1 tbsp. coriander leaves and thinly sliced red spur chilli

PREPARATION :

1. Wash the crabs and then steam them whole. When done, remove all the meat. You may save the shells for stuffing.

2. Knead together the crabmeat, pork, coriander root, garlic, pepper, soy sauce, salt, and one egg. When well mixed, pack this filling into cup or crab shells, steam until done. Allow it to cool, then remove the filling out of the cups. (In case the crab shells are used, do not remove the filling.)

3. Pour the oil into a frying pan and place on medium heat.

4. Beat the remaining egg well add the beaten egg onto the exposed surface of the crab filling, and then sprinkle with breadcrumb.

5. When the oil is hot, put the filling into it, until the filling turns golden brown, lift the filling from the oil, drain, garnish with coriander leaves and chilli shreds, and serve with chilli sauce. (Puja can be served steamed as well as fried)

4 Serving

เครื่องปรุง

ปูเนื้อล้างสะอาด 3 ตัว
หมูสับ 1 ถ้วย
รากผักชีโขลก 1/2 ช้อนโต๊ะ
กระเทียมโขลก 1 ช้อนชา
พริกไทยป่น 1/4 ช้อนชา ซีอิ๊วขาว 1 1/2 ช้อนโต๊ะ
เกลือ 1/4 ช้อนชา ไข่ไก่ 2 ฟอง
ขนมปังป่น 3 ช้อนโต๊ะ
น้ำมันพืช 2 ถ้วย
ใบผักชีและพริกชี้ฟ้าหั่นฝอย 1 ช้อนโต๊ะ

วิธีทำ

1. นึ่งปูแกะเอาแต่เนื้อ (จะล้างกระดองปูเก็บไว้ก็ได้)

2. นวดเนื้อปูกับหมู รากผักชี กระเทียม พริกไทย ซีอิ๊ว เกลือ และไข่ 1 ฟอง จนเป็นเนื้อเดียวกัน ตักใส่ถ้วยหรือจะนำไปใส่กระดองปูก็ได้ นำไปนึ่งจนสุก ปล่อยไว้ให้เย็น แล้วแกะออกจากถ้วย ถ้าบรรจุในกระดองปูก็ไม่ต้องแกะออก

3. ตีไข่อีก 1 ฟอง ไว้ชุบปูจ๋า (ถ้าเป็นกระดองปูก็จุ่มแต่ส่วนหน้า) แล้ว คลุกขนมปังป่นอีกชั้นหนึ่ง

4. ตั้งกระทะไฟกลางรองจนน้ำมันร้อนทอดปูจ๋า (ถ้าอยู่ในกระดองปู ก็ทอด แบบคว่ำหน้า) เมื่อเหลืองดีแล้วตักขึ้นให้สะเด็ดน้ำมัน รับประทานกับซอสพริก (อาจรับประทานเมื่อนึ่งสุกโดยไม่ต้องนำมาทอดอีกก็ได้)

PIK KAI SOT SAI THOT
(Fried Stuffed Chicken Wings)
ปีกไก่สอดไส้ทอด

INGREDIENTS :

6 chicken wings, deboned
1/2 cup mungbean noodles, soaked in warm water for 15 minutes and then cut into 1/2 inch pieces
1 tbsp. chopped coriander greens
1/2 cup sliced water chestnuts
1 tsp. salt
1 tbsp. light soy sauce
2 eggs
1 tbsp. chopped garlic
1/3 cup wheat flour
1 1/2 cups ground pork
1 cup breadcrumbs
3 cups cooking oil

PREPARATION :

1. Mix together the noodles, coriander, chestnuts, one egg, garlic, 2 tbsp. flour, ground pork, salt and soy sauce and stuff this mixture into the chicken wings (not too full).

2. Steam the chicken wings for 15 minutes; then, drain and cool.

3. Dredge chicken wings with the remaining flour. Beat the egg well. Dip the wings in the egg and then in the breadcrumbs. Deep fry them until golden brown.

4. Serve with sweet chilli sauce (See p.139)

3-4 Serving

เครื่องปรุง

ปีกไก่เลาะเอากระดูกออก 6 ปีก
วุ้นเส้นแช่น้ำให้นุ่ม หั่นเป็นท่อนยาว 1/2 นิ้ว 1/2 ถ้วย
ผักชีหั่นละเอียด 1 ช้อนโต๊ะ
แห้วฝานเป็นชิ้นบางๆ 1/2 ถ้วย
เกลือ 1 ช้อนชา ซีอิ๊ว 1 ช้อนโต๊ะ
ไข่ไก่ 2 ฟอง
กระเทียมสับละเอียด 1 ช้อนโต๊ะ
แป้งสาลี 1/3 ถ้วย หมูสับ 1 1/2 ถ้วย
ผงขนมปัง 1 ถ้วย
น้ำมันพืชสำหรับทอดปีกไก่ 3 ถ้วย

วิธีทำ

1. คลุกวุ้นเส้น ผักชี แห้ว ไข่ 1 ฟอง กระเทียม แป้ง 2 ช้อนโต๊ะ หมูสับ เกลือ ซีอิ๊ว เข้าด้วยกันใช้เป็นไส้ ยัดไส้เข้าในปีกไก่อย่าให้แน่นเกินไป

2. แล้วนึ่งปีกไก่ประมาณ 15 นาที ทิ้งไว้ให้สะเด็ดน้ำ คลุกปีกไก่กับแป้งสาลีที่เหลือ ตีไข่ให้เข้ากัน จุ่มปีกไก่ลงในไข่ แล้วจึงคลุกผงขนมปังให้ทั่ว

3. ใส่น้ำมันลงในกระทะลึก พอร้อนใส่ปีกไก่ทอดให้เหลือง ตักขึ้นให้สะเด็ดน้ำมัน ซับน้ำมันให้แห้ง

4. เสิร์ฟกับซอสพริกหวาน (ดูหน้า 139)

THOT MAN PLA
(Fried Fish Cakes)
ทอดมันปลา

INGREDIENTS :

500 grams white fish meat (e.g. ladyfinger), minced or chopped
1 tbsp. red curry paste (See p. 22)
1 egg
1/2 cup yard-long beans, sliced fine
3 tbsp. kaffir lime leaves, minced or chopped
1 tsp. salt
1 tsp. sugar
3 cups vegetable oil

PREPARATION :

1. Put all the ingredients in a large bowl and mix well with the hand.

2. Spoon the mixture 2 tbsp. ; shape into small patties about 3" in diameter and deep fry in vegetable oil until golden brown.

3. Serve with peanut sweet chilli sauce.

PEANUT SWEET CHILLI SAUCE

Use cucumber relish (see p. 157)   and add 1/4 cup sliced shallot and 1/2 cup freshly ground peanuts.

4 Serving

เครื่องปรุง

เนื้อปลาขูด 500 กรัม
น้ำพริกแกงแดง (ดูหน้า 22) 1 ช้อนโต๊ะ
ไข่ไก่ 1 ฟอง
ถั่วฝักยาวหั่นละเอียด 1/2 ถ้วย
ใบมะกรูดซอย 3 ช้อนโต๊ะ
เกลือ 1 ช้อนชา น้ำตาลทราย 1 ช้อนชา
น้ำมันพืชสำหรับทอด 3 ถ้วย

วิธีทำ

1. ผสมเครื่องปรุงทั้งหมดเข้าด้วยกัน ใช้มือนวด

2. ปั้นส่วนผสมขึ้นมาเป็นก้อนประมาณ 2 ช้อนโต๊ะแล้วแผ่เป็นแผ่นกลม เส้นผ่าศูนย์กลางประมาณ 3 นิ้ว ทอดในน้ำมันร้อน ไฟแรงปานกลาง จน สุกเหลืองดี ตักขึ้นพักไว้ให้สะเด็ดน้ำมัน

3. เสิร์ฟกับน้ำจิ้ม ใช้อาจาด (ดูหน้า 157)

THOT MAN KHAO PHOT
(Fried Sweet Corn Patties)
ทอดมันข้าวโพด

INGREDIENTS :

2 cups sweet corn kernels
1/4 tsp. pepper
1 tsp. salt
2 tsp. well-pounded garlic
2 tsp. wheat flour
1 egg
2 cups cooking oil

PREPARATION :

1. Knead together well the corn, pepper, salt, garlic, egg, and flour to obtain a stiff dough.
2. Place the oil in a wok over medium heat. When the oil is hot, pick up about 1 tbsp. of the dough, shape into a patty with the fingers, and place the patty in the oil. Continue making patties and putting them in but do not crowd the wok. Turn as needed so the patties brown on both sides; then, remove from the oil and drain on absorbent paper.
3. Serve with chilli sauce or catsup.

4 Serving

เครื่องปรุง

ข้าวโพดฝานเอาแต่เนื้อ 2 ถ้วย
พริกไทย 1/4 ช้อนชา
เกลือ 1 ช้อนชา
กระเทียมโขลกละเอียด 2 ช้อนชา
แป้งสาลี 2 ช้อนชา
ไข่ไก่ 1 ฟอง
น้ำมันพืชสำหรับทอด 2 ถ้วย

วิธีทำ

1. นวดข้าวโพด พริกไทย เกลือ กระเทียม แป้ง และไข่ให้เข้ากัน
2. ตักข้าวโพดที่ผสมปั้นเป็นก้อนกลม ใส่น้ำมันลงในกระทะลึก พอน้ำมันร้อนใช้ไฟแรงปานกลาง ใส่ข้าวโพดทอดจนสุกเหลืองดี ตักขึ้นพักให้สะเด็ดน้ำมัน
3. เสิร์ฟกับซอสพริกหรือซอสมะเขือเทศ

NEUA DAET DIAO
(Fried Sun-Dried Beef)
เนื้อแดดเดียว

INGREDIENTS :

400 grams round beef
1 garlic bulb
3 coriander roots
1/2 tsp. pepper
1 tbsp. fish sauce
1 tbsp. oyster sauce
2 tbsp. whiskey
1 tbsp. sugar
1 tsp. curry powder

PREPARATION :

1. After washing the beef, cut it into slices about 1/3 inch thick.

2. Pound the garlic, coriander root, and pepper in a mortar. Add the beef slices and work them around in the mixture. Add the fish sauce, oyster sauce, whiskey, sugar and curry powder, mix well, and allow to marinate for one hour.

3. Arrange the slices of beef on a rack and leave in the sun for 4 hours. Turn occasionally.

4. Fry the sun-dried beef in hot oil and then drain.

4 Serving

เครื่องปรุง

เนื้อวัว 400 กรัม
กระเทียม 1 หัว รากผักชี 3 ราก
พริกไทย 1/2 ช้อนชา น้ำปลา 1 ช้อนโต๊ะ
ซอสน้ำมันหอย 1 ช้อนโต๊ะ
วิสกี้ 2 ช้อนโต๊ะ
น้ำตาลทราย 1 ช้อนโต๊ะ
ผงกะหรี่ 1 ช้อนชา

วิธีทำ

1. ล้างเนื้อ หั่นเป็นชิ้นหนาประมาณ 1/3 นิ้ว

2. โขลกกระเทียม รากผักชี และพริกไทยให้ละเอียด ใส่เนื้อลงคลุก เติม น้ำปลา ซอสน้ำมันหอย วิสกี้ น้ำตาลทรายและผงกะหรี่ลงไปคลุกให้เข้ากัน หมักทิ้งไว้ 1 ชั่วโมง

3. เรียงชิ้นเนื้อบนตะแกรง ตากแดดจัดๆ 4 ชั่วโมง กลับด้านตากบ้าง

4. นำเนื้อที่ตากแล้วมาทอด พักให้สะเด็ดน้ำมันก่อนเสิร์ฟ

PHAT MU PRIAO WAN
(Stir-Fried Sweet and Sour Pork)
ผัดหมูเปรี้ยวหวาน

INGREDIENTS :

400 grams lean pork, sliced into thin 2" × 1" strips
1 tbsp. vegetable oil
1/2 cup cucumber cut into bite-sized pieces
1 tsp. chopped garlic
100 grams straw mushrooms, sliced
1 large tomato, sliced
1 cup 1-inch lengths of spring onion
2 spur chillies, sliced
1/3 cup sliced onion
1 tbsp. vinegar
2 tbsp. tomato sauce
2 tbsp. sugar
1 tbsp. fish sauce
1/4 tsp. salt
1/2 cup chicken stock
1 tbsp. tapioca flour
1/4 tbsp. pepper
1 tbsp. coriander leaves

PREPARATION :

1. Heat oil in wok over medium-high heat and brown the garlic. Add the pork and cook for 5 minutes, stirring constantly. Then, add the cucumber, mushrooms, tomato, spring onion, onion, chilli, vinegar, tomato sauce, sugar, fish sauce, salt and half of the chicken stock. Stir well.

2. Mix the remaining chicken stock with the tapioca flour, blend well and pour slowly into the wok and cook until the sauce thickens. Remove from heat and season with peper. Garnish with coriander.

4 Serving

เครื่องปรุง

หมูเนื้อสันหั่นเป็นชิ้น 2 นิ้ว × 1 นิ้ว 400 กรัม
น้ำมันพืช 1 ช้อนโต๊ะ
แตงกวาสดหั่นเป็นชิ้นเล็กพอคำ 1/2 ถ้วย
กระเทียมสับละเอียด 1 ช้อนชา
เห็ดฟางหั่นเป็นชิ้น 100 กรัม
มะเขือเทศขนาดใหญ่หั่นเป็นชิ้นเล็ก 1 ผล
ต้นหอมหั่นเป็นท่อนขนาด 1 นิ้ว 1 ถ้วย
พริกชี้ฟ้าเอาเมล็ดออกหั่นเฉลบ 2 เม็ด
หอมใหญ่หั่นเป็นแว่น 1/3 ถ้วย
น้ำส้มสายชู 1 ช้อนโต๊ะ ซอสมะเขือเทศ 2 ช้อนโต๊ะ
น้ำตาล 2 ช้อนโต๊ะ น้ำปลา 1 ช้อนโต๊ะ
เกลือ 1/4 ช้อนชา น้ำต้มกระดูก 1/2 ถ้วย
แป้งมัน 1 ช้อนโต๊ะ พริกไทยป่น 1/4 ช้อนโต๊ะ
ผักชีเด็ดเป็นใบ 1 ช้อนโต๊ะ

วิธีทำ

1. ตั้งน้ำมันใช้ไฟค่อนข้างแรง เจียวกระเทียมแล้วใส่หมูลงไปผัดประมาณ 5 นาที แล้วใส่แตงกวา เห็ด มะเขือเทศ ต้นหอม พริก หอมใหญ่ ปรุงรสด้วยน้ำส้มสายชู ซอสมะเขือเทศ น้ำตาล น้ำปลา เกลือ แล้วเติมน้ำต้มกระดูกลงไปครึ่งหนึ่ง

2. ผสมน้ำต้มกระดูกที่เหลือกับแป้งมันสำปะหลัง ให้แป้งละลายดีแล้วริน ใส่ในกระทะ ผัดต่อสักครู่ เมื่อน้ำแกงข้นแล้วตักขึ้นโรยพริกไทย แต่งด้วยผักชี

PHAT PLA MEUK YAT SAI
(Stir-Fried Stuffed Squid)
ผัดปลาหมึกยัดไส้

INGREDIENTS FOR FILLING :

200 grams ground pork
1 tsp. chopped coriander root
1/4 tsp. pepper
1 tbsp. chopped garlic
1 tbsp. chopped onion
1 tbsp. fish sauce
1 tbsp. light soy sauce
1 tsp. sugar
1 egg (slightly beaten)

OTHER INGREDIENTS :

6-8 medium sized fresh whole squids
1 tsp. minced garlic
1/4 cup vegetable oil
2 tbsp. sliced fresh ginger
1/2 cup sliced Shiitake mushroom
1 tbsp. oyster sauce
1/4 cup water

PREPARATION :

1. Clean the squid and set aside. In a bowl, mix the ingredients for the filling by hand. Stuff this filling into the whole squid and steam for 15 minutes. Then, cut diagonally into slices.

2. Heat oil in a wok. Fry the garlic until fragrant, then add the slices of stuffed squid and the rest of the ingredients. Fry for 5 minutes and dip onto a plate.

4 Serving

เครื่องปรุงไส้

หมูสับ 200 กรัม
รากผักชีโขลก 1 ช้อนชา
พริกไทยป่น 1/4 ช้อนชา กระเทียมสับ 1 ช้อนโต๊ะ
หอมใหญ่สับละเอียด 1 ช้อนโต๊ะ
น้ำปลา 1 ช้อนโต๊ะ ซีอิ๊วขาว 1 ช้อนโต๊ะ
น้ำตาลทราย 1 ช้อนชา ไข่ (ตีเบาๆ) 1 ฟอง

เครื่องปรุงอื่น ๆ

ปลาหมึกขนาดกลาง 6-8 ตัว
กระเทียมสับ 1 ช้อนชา น้ำมันพืช 1/4 ถ้วย
ขิงฝานเป็นแว่นบาง 2 ช้อนโต๊ะ
เห็ดหอมแช่น้ำหั่นบาง ๆ 1/2 ถ้วย
น้ำมันหอย 1 ช้อนโต๊ะ น้ำ 1/4 ถ้วย

วิธีทำ

1. ล้างปลาหมึกให้สะอาด ใช้มือคลุกผสมเครื่องปรุงไส้ทั้งหมดเข้าด้วยกัน แล้วยัดเป็นไส้ปลาหมึก

2. นึ่งปลาหมึกราว 15 นาที ทิ้งไว้ให้เย็นแล้วหั่นตามขวางเป็นแว่น ๆ

3. เจียวกระเทียมให้หอม แล้วใส่ปลาหมึกลงผัดกับเครื่องปรุงอื่น ๆ ที่เหลือ ประมาณ 5 นาที ตักขึ้น

PHAT NEUA NAMMAN HOI
(Stir-Fried Beef in Oyster Sauce)
ผัดเนื้อน้ำมันหอย

INGREDIENTS :

400 grams thin slices of tender beef
1 tbsp. wheat flour
2 tbsp. light soy sauce
3 tbsp. cooking oil
1 tbsp. chopped garlic
3 Shiitake mushrooms, soaked in water and sliced
200 grams straw mushrooms or champignons
4 tbsp. oyster sauce
1 tsp. sugar
1/2 tsp. pepper
2 spring onion cut into short lengths
1 red spur chilli, sliced

PREPARATION :

1. Marinate the beef slices in a mixture of the flour and light soy sauce.

2. Place the oil in a wok over medium heat. Fry the garlic until fragrant and then add the Shiitake mushrooms, and straw mushrooms. When the mushroom is tender, put in the beef and continue stir-frying until it is done.

3. Add the oyster sauce, sugar, and pepper, stir to mix well, add the spring onion and spur chilli, stir again; then, dip onto a platter and serve right away.

3-4 Serving

เครื่องปรุง

เนื้อสันในวัวหั่นเป็นชิ้นยาว 400 กรัม
แป้งสาลี 1 ช้อนโต๊ะ
ซีอิ๊วขาว 2 ช้อนโต๊ะ น้ำมันพืช 3 ช้อนโต๊ะ
กระเทียมสับ 1 ช้อนโต๊ะ
เห็ดหอมแช่น้ำหั่นบาง 3 ดอก
เห็ดฟาง หรือซองปิยอง 200 กรัม
ซอสน้ำมันหอย 4 ช้อนโต๊ะ น้ำตาล 1 ช้อนชา
พริกไทย 1/2 ช้อนชา
ต้นหอม หั่นเป็นท่อนสั้น ๆ 2 ต้น
พริกชี้ฟ้าแดงหั่นแฉลบ 1 เม็ด

วิธีทำ

1. ผสมแป้งสาลีกับซีอิ๊วขาว หมักเนื้อไว้

2. ใส่น้ำมันลงกระทะไฟแรงปานกลาง เจียวกระเทียมให้เหลืองหอม ใส่เห็ดหอมและเห็ดฟางลงไปผัดพอสุก ใส่เนื้อลงผัดจนเนื้อสุก

3. ใส่ซอสน้ำมันหอย น้ำตาล และพริกไทย คนให้เข้ากัน ใส่ต้นหอมและพริกชี้ฟ้าแดง ลงไปผัดอีกครั้ง แล้วตักขึ้นเสิร์ฟทันที

KUNG PHAT SOM MAKHAM PIAK
(Stir-Fried Prawns in Tamarind Sauce)
กุ้งผัดส้มมะขามเปียก

INGREDIENTS:

500 grams jumbo prawns shelled and deveined
2 tbsp. chopped onion
2 tbsp. vegetable oil
2 tbsp. chicken broth or water
2 tbsp. palm sugar
1/3 cup tamarind juice
1 tbsp. fish sauce
7 fried, dried red chillies
1 tbsp. fried minced garlic
2 tbsp. fried sliced shallot
1/3 cup chopped spring onion
1 red bell pepper

PREPARATION:

1. Put the vegetable oil in a wok over medium heat. Brown the onion, and add the palm sugar, chicken broth, tamarind juice, fish sauce and chillies, stirring and turning with a spatula.
2. When the liquid begins to boil, add the prawns, garlic and shallot, and remove when prawns are done.
3. Garnish with red bell pepper.

2 Serving

KUNG KRA THIAM
(Garlic Prawn)
กุ้งกระเทียม

INGREDIENTS:

8-12 jumbo prawns, shelled and deveined
2 tbsp. chopped garlic
1 tsp. pepper
1/2 tbsp. fish sauce
1 1/4 tsp. sugar
1 tbsp. chopped coriander root
4 tbsp. vegetable oil
1/2 cup chopped spring onion
1/4 cup chopped or minced ginger

PREPARATION:

In a wok or big frying pan, heat the oil over high heat. Fry the garlic, coriander root, pepper, sugar, fish sauce and prawns, stirring constantly. Cook for 2 minutes and then add the remaining ingredients, stir well, and remove from heat.

2 Serving

เครื่องปรุง

กุ้งก้ามกรามขนาดใหญ่ปอกเปลือกชักเส้นดำออก 500 กรัม
หอมใหญ่หั่นละเอียด 2 ช้อนโต๊ะ น้ำมันพืช 2 ช้อนโต๊ะ
น้ำหรือน้ำต้มกระดูกไก่ 2 ช้อนโต๊ะ
น้ำตาลปีบ 2 ช้อนโต๊ะ น้ำส้มมะขาม 1/3 ถ้วย
น้ำปลา 2 ช้อนโต๊ะ พริกขี้หนูแห้งทอดน้ำมัน 7 เม็ด
กระเทียมซอย เจียวแล้ว 1 ช้อนโต๊ะ
หอมแดงซอย เจียวแล้ว 2 ช้อนโต๊ะ
พริกชี้ฟ้าแดง 1 เม็ด

วิธีทำ

1. เจียวหอมใหญ่ในน้ำมัน ใช้ไฟปานกลาง จนเหลือง หอม แล้วเติมน้ำตาล น้ำต้มกระดูก น้ำส้มมะขาม น้ำปลา และพริกลงไป ผัดคลุกให้เข้ากันจน ส่วนผสมเดือด
2. ใส่กุ้ง กระเทียมเจียว หอมเจียว
3. กุ้งสุก ตักใส่จาน แต่งด้วยพริกชี้ฟ้าแดง

เครื่องปรุง

กุ้งก้ามกรามขนาดใหญ่. ปอกเปลือก ชักเส้นดำออก 8-12 ตัว
กระเทียมสับละเอียด 2 ช้อนโต๊ะ
พริกไทยป่น 1 ช้อนชา
น้ำปลา 1/2 ช้อนโต๊ะ น้ำตาลทราย 1 1/4 ช้อนชา
รากผักชีสับละเอียด 1 ช้อนโต๊ะ น้ำมันพืช 4 ช้อนโต๊ะ
ต้นหอมซอย 1/2 ถ้วย ขิงซอย 1/4 ถ้วย

วิธีทำ

เจียวกระเทียม รากผักชี พริกไทย ให้หอม ใช้ไฟแรง เติมน้ำตาล น้ำปลา ลงไป ใส่กุ้ง หมั่นคน ตั้งไฟนานประมาณ 2 นาที แล้วใส่ต้นหอมกับขิง คนให้เข้ากันแล้วยกลง

PHAT KAI KAP MET MAMUANG HIMAPHAN

(Stir-Fried Chicken with Cashew Nut)

ผัดไก่กับเม็ดมะม่วงหิมพานต์

INGREDIENTS :

300 grams sliced chicken breast
2 tbsp. vegetable oil
1/2 tbsp. chopped garlic
1/2 cup freshly roasted cashew nuts
1/4 cup thinly sliced fried dried chillies
1 small onion, sliced
1/3 cup spring onion, cut into short lengths
1 1/2 tbsp. fish sauce
1 tbsp. dark soy sauce 1/4 tsp. salt
1 red spur chilli, sliced
4-5 coriander leaves

PREPARATION :

Heat oil in wok over medium heat. Fry the garlic. When it has yellowed, add the chicken and cook for 3 minutes, turning regularly. Then, add the cashew nuts, chillies, onion, spring onion, fish sauce, dark soy sauce, and salt and cook for 4 minutes. Garnish with the spring onion, chilli and coriander leaves.

4 Serving

เครื่องปรุง

เนื้อไก่ส่วนอกหั่นเป็นชิ้นบาง 300 กรัม
น้ำมันพืช 2 ช้อนโต๊ะ
กระเทียมสับละเอียด 1/2 ช้อนโต๊ะ
เม็ดมะม่วงหิมพานต์ดิบ 1/2 ถ้วย
พริกแห้งทอดหั่นฝอย 1/4 ถ้วย
หอมใหญ่ขนาดเล็กหั่นเป็นชิ้นเล็ก 1 หัว
ต้นหอมหั่นเป็นท่อน 1/3 ถ้วย น้ำปลา 1 1/2 ช้อนโต๊ะ
ซีอิ๊วดำ 1 ช้อนโต๊ะ เกลือ 1/4 ช้อนชา
พริกชี้ฟ้าแดงหั่นแฉลบ 1 เม็ด ใบผักชี 4-5 ใบ

วิธีทำ

ใส่น้ำมันในกระทะ ตั้งไฟแรงปานกลาง เมื่อน้ำมันร้อนเจียวกระเทียมให้เหลืองหอม ใส่เนื้อไก่ลงผัด 3 นาที แล้วใส่เม็ดมะม่วงหิมพานต์ พริก หอม ต้นหอม ปรุงรสด้วยน้ำปลา ซีอิ๊วดำ และเกลือ ผัดต่ออีก 4 นาที ตักใส่จานโรยด้วยต้นหอมพริกชี้ฟ้าและใบผักชี

PHAT PHAK ANAMAI
(Stir-Fried Prawns with Vegetables)
ผัดผักอนามัย

INGREDIENTS :

12 prawns
1 young sponge gourd
10 baby corns
10 rice-straw mushrooms or champignons
3 tbsp. cooking oil
1 tbsp. chopped garlic
3 tbsp. oyster sauce
1/4 tsp. salt

PREPARATION :

1. Peel and wash the sponge gourd and cut into bite-sized pieces. Slice the baby corn and rice-straw mushrooms in half. If champignons are used, scald them before slicing. Shell and devein the prawns.

2. Heat the oil in a wok. When it is hot, put in the garlic. When the garlic is fragrant, add the prawns and salt. When the prawns are done, add the baby corn and then the mushrooms. When the mushrooms are done, add the sponge gourd and fry until cooked. Add the oyster sauce and stir thoroughly; then, dip up onto a platter and serve hot.

4 Serving

เครื่องปรุง

กุ้งนางแกะเปลือก ชักเส้นดำออก 12 ตัว
บวบ 1 ผล ข้าวโพดอ่อน 10 ฝัก
เห็ดฟางหรือซองปิยอง 10 ดอก
น้ำมันพืช 3 ช้อนโต๊ะ
กระเทียมสับละเอียด 1 ช้อนโต๊ะ
ซอสน้ำมันหอย 3 ช้อนโต๊ะ
เกลือ 1/4 ช้อนชา

วิธีทำ

1. ปอกเปลือกบวบแล้วล้าง หั่นเป็นชิ้นขนาดพอคำ หั่นข้าวโพดอ่อน ผ่าครึ่ง เห็ดฟาง หากใช้เห็ดซองปิยองให้ลวกก่อนนำมาผ่าครึ่ง

2. ใส่น้ำมันในกระทะ ตั้งไฟจนน้ำมันร้อนดี เจียวกระเทียมให้เหลืองหอม แล้วใส่กุ้งกับเกลือลงไปผัดพอสุก

3. ใส่ข้าวโพดอ่อนและเห็ดลงไปผัดพอสุกใส่บวบลงผัดพอสุก เติมซอส น้ำมันหอย คนให้เข้ากัน แล้วตักใส่จาน เสิร์ฟร้อน ๆ

PHAT KHA-NA NAMMAN HOI
(Stir-Fried Kale in Oyster Sauce)
ผัดคะน้าน้ำมันหอย

INGREDIENTS :

10 kale plants (or kai lan plants) of equal size
20 rice-straw mushrooms, or champignons
3 tbsp. cooking oil
1 tbsp. finely chopped garlic
4 tbsp. oyster sauce
1/4 tsp. salt
1/4 tsp. pepper 1 tsp. sugar

PREPARATION :

1. Wash the kale (or kai lan) well, remove the old leaves, the old part of the stem, and the tough outer covering of the stem.

2. Wash the mushrooms and remove any inedible portions.

3. To boiling water, add 1 tsp. salt. Parboil kale; remove from hot water immediately and submerge in cold water. Scald the mushrooms in a similar manner. Drain both the kale and the mushrooms.

4. Heat the oil in a wok. When it is hot, fry the garlic. When it is fragrant, add the kale and mushrooms, stir to mix well, and then add the chicken stock, oyster sauce, sugar, and pepper. Stir well; then spoon into a platter and serve hot.

4 Serving

เครื่องปรุง

ผักคะน้าต้นขนาดเท่า ๆ กัน 10 ต้น
เห็ดฟางหรือซองปิยอง 20 ดอก น้ำมันพืช 3 ช้อนโต๊ะ
กระเทียมสับละเอียด 1 ช้อนโต๊ะ
ซอสน้ำมันหอย 4 ช้อนโต๊ะ เกลือ 1/4 ช้อนชา
พริกไทย 1/4 ช้อนชา น้ำตาล 1 ช้อนชา

วิธีทำ

1. ล้างผักคะน้าให้สะอาด ตัดใบแก่และก้านส่วนที่แข็งทิ้ง

2. เห็ด แต่งแล้วล้างให้สะอาด

3. ต้มน้ำให้เดือด ใส่เกลือลงไป 1 ช้อนชา จุ่มต้นคะน้าลงเอาโคนลงก่อน เมื่อคะน้าเปลี่ยนสีเป็นสีสุกให้ตักออก แช่น้ำเย็นทันที ลวกเห็ดด้วยวิธีเดียวกัน แล้วพักให้สะเด็ดน้ำ

4. ใส่น้ำมันในกระทะ เจียวกระเทียมให้เหลืองหอม ใส่คะน้าและเห็ดลงไป ผัด เติมน้ำต้มกระดูกไก่ เกลือ ซอสน้ำมันหอย น้ำตาล พริกไทย คนให้เข้ากัน ตักขึ้นเสิร์ฟ

PU PHAT PHONG KARI
(Stir-Fried Crab in Curry Sauce)
ปูผัดผงกะหรี่

INGREDIENTS :

1 roe crab
1 onion
2 celery plants
3 spring onions
2 red spur chillies
1/4 tsp. pepper
2 tsp. curry powder
1/2 cup milk
1 tbsp. roasted chilli paste
1 egg
2 tbsp. oyster sauce

PREPARATION

1. Wash the crab, remove the shell, chop into pieces, and crack the claws and legs.

2. Heat 2 tbsp. oil in a frying pan. When it is hot, put in the crab, fry until done, and then add the curry powder.

3. Mix the milk and the chilli paste and then beat in the egg. Pour this into the pan and add the oyster sauce.

4. Chop the onion, celery, spur chilli, and spring onion, add these to the mixture in the pan, sprinkle with pepper, and continue cooking until done; then, dip onto a dish and serve.

2-3 Serving

เครื่องปรุง

ปูไข่ 1 ตัว
หอมใหญ่ 1 หัว
ขึ้นฉ่าย 2 ต้น
ต้นหอม 3 ต้น
พริกชี้ฟ้าแดง 2 เม็ด
พริกไทยป่น 1/4 ช้อนชา
ผงกะหรี่ 2 ช้อนชา
นมสด 1/2 ถ้วย
น้ำพริกเผา 1 ช้อนโต๊ะ
ไข่ไก่ 1 ฟอง
น้ำมันหอย 2 ช้อนโต๊ะ

วิธีทำ

1. ล้างปูให้สะอาด สับเป็นชิ้น

2. ใส่น้ำมันในกระทะ พอน้ำมันร้อนใส่ปูลงผัดจนปูสุก จึงใส่ผงกะหรี่

3. ผสมนมสด น้ำพริกเผา และไข่ไก่ตีให้เข้ากัน แล้วเทใส่ลงในกระทะ เติมน้ำมันหอย

4. ใส่หอมใหญ่ ขึ้นฉ่าย พริกชี้ฟ้าแดง ต้นหอมหั่น ผัดให้เข้ากันจนสุก โรยพริกไทยป่น ตักขึ้นใส่จานเสิร์ฟได้

PHAT KHI MAO KAI
(Spicy Stir-Fried Chicken)
ผัดขี้เมาไก่

INGREDIENTS :

2 cups ground chicken
15 cloves garlic
5 hot chillies
4 coriander roots
2 tbsp. cooking oil
1 tbsp. oyster sauce
2 tbsp. fish sauce
1 tsp. sugar
1/4 cup chicken stock
1/2 cup holy basil leaves (ka-prao)
1 sliced red spur chilli

PREPARATION :

1. Pound the garlic, chillies, and coriander roots well in a mortar.

2. Heat the oil in a wok. When the oil is hot, add the pounded chilli mixture and fry with stirring. When the garlic is golden, add the meat and continue stirring and turning.

3. When the meat is done, add the oyster sauce, fish sauce, sugar, and chicken stock to give the dish some liquid. Add the basil leaves and chilli, and stir to mis; then serve with rice.

4 Serving

เครื่องปรุง

เนื้อไก่บดหรือสับ 2 ถ้วย
กระเทียม 15 กลีบ
พริกขี้หนู 5 เม็ด รากผักชี 4 ราก
น้ำมันพืช 2 ช้อนโต๊ะ
ซอสน้ำมันหอย 1 ช้อนโต๊ะ น้ำปลา 2 ช้อนโต๊ะ
น้ำตาล 1 ช้อนชา
น้ำต้มกระดูกไก่ 1/4 ถ้วย
ใบกะเพรา 1/2 ถ้วย
พริกชี้ฟ้าแดงหั่นเฉลบ 1 เม็ด

วิธีทำ

1. โขลกกระเทียม พริก และรากผักชีให้ละเอียด

2. ตั้งกระทะ ใส่น้ำมัน พอน้ำมันร้อนดี ใส่กระเทียม พริกและรากผักชี โขลกลงไปผัดจนหอม ใส่เนื้อไก่ลงไปผัดต่อ

3. เมื่อเนื้อไก่สุก ใส่ซอสน้ำมันหอย น้ำปลา น้ำตาล และเติมน้ำต้มกระดูก ไก่ลงไปเพื่อไม่ให้แห้ง ใส่กะเพราและพริกคนพอทั่ว ตักขึ้น

PHAT PHET MU
(Stir-Fried Pork with Red Curry Paste)
ผัดเผ็ดหมู

INGREDIENTS :

400 grams lean pork sliced into thin strips about 1 inch wide and 2 inches long
1 tbsp. red curry paste (See p. 22)
1 tbsp. vegetable oil
1 cup coconut milk
1 1/2 tbsp. fish sauce
1/4 tsp. salt
1/2 tbsp. sugar
3-5 kaffir lime leaves
2 fresh red chillies, sliced
3 green pepper

PREPARATION :

1. Heat oil in wok over medium heat. Fry the red curry paste and pork for 5 minutes, stirring regularly. Add half of the coconut milk and cook for another 10 minutes, stirring occasionally.

2. When the pork is done, add the remaining coconut milk, the fish sauce, kaffir lime leaves, salt and sugar, stir well and bring to a boil

3. Then, add chillies, and stir well. Spoon onto a plate.

4 Serving

เครื่องปรุง

หมูเนื้อสันหั่นเป็นชิ้นบางกว้างยาว 1 นิ้ว 400 กรัม
น้ำพริกแกงแดง (ดูหน้า 22) 1 ช้อนโต๊ะ
น้ำมันพืช 1 ช้อนโต๊ะ
กะทิ 1 ถ้วย น้ำปลา 1 1/2 ช้อนโต๊ะ
เกลือ 1/4 ช้อนชา น้ำตาล 1/2 ช้อนโต๊ะ
ใบมะกรูด 3-5 ใบ
พริกชี้ฟ้าแดง หั่นแฉลบ 2 เม็ด พริกไทยอ่อน 3 ช่อ

วิธีทำ

1. ใส่น้ำมันในกระทะไฟปานกลาง พอน้ำมันร้อนผัดน้ำพริกให้หอม ใส่หมูลงไปผัดประมาณ 5 นาที ใส่กะทิลงไปครึ่งหนึ่ง แล้วตั้งไฟต่อประมาณ 10 นาที หมั่นคน

2. เมื่อเนื้อหมูสุกเติมกะทิที่เหลือลงไป ปรุงรสด้วยน้ำปลา เกลือ น้ำตาล ใส่ใบมะกรูด คนให้เข้ากันตั้งไฟต่อจนเดือด

3. ใส่พริก คนให้เข้ากัน ตักขึ้นเสิร์ฟ

PHAT PHRIK KHING KAI
(Savory Stir-Fried Chicken)
ผัดพริกขิงไก่

INGREDIENTS :

500 grams sliced chicken breast
1 tbsp. phrik khing curry paste (See p. 71)
1/2 cup coconut milk
3 tbsp. vegetable oil
2 tbsp. fish sauce
1 tbsp. sugar
4 kaffir lime leaves, minced

PREPARATION :

Put oil into a wok over a medium heat. Add the phrik khing curry paste and stir well. Next add the coconut milk and chicken, stirring regularly until the chicken is done. Then add the kaffir lime leaves, fish sauce, and sugar to taste. Remove from the heat and sprinkle with minced kaffir lime leaves and chilli.

4 *Serving*

เครื่องปรุง

เนื้อไก่ส่วนอกหั่นเป็นชิ้นเล็ก 500 กรัม
น้ำพริกผัดพริกขิง (ดูหน้า 71) 1 ช้อนโต๊ะ
กะทิ 1/2 ถ้วย
น้ำมันพืช 3 ช้อนโต๊ะ
น้ำปลา 2 ช้อนโต๊ะ
น้ำตาล 1 ช้อนโต๊ะ
ใบมะกรูดหั่นฝอย 4 ใบ

วิธีทำ

ตั้งกระทะบนไฟแรงปานกลาง ใส่น้ำมัน เมื่อน้ำมันร้อนดีแล้วใส่น้ำพริก ลงไปผัดให้หอม ใส่กะทิลงไปคนพอเดือดใส่เนื้อไก่ลงไปผัดจนเนื้อไก่สุก ปรุงรสด้วยน้ำปลา น้ำตาล ตักใส่จานโรยด้วยใบมะกรูด

PHAT PHRIK KHING MU KAP THUA FAK YAO
(Savory Stir-Fried Pork with Yard-long Beans)
ผัดพริกขิงหมูกับถั่วฝักยาว

INGREDIENTS FOR CHILLI PASTE :

3 dried chillies
7 shallots
2 garlic bulbs
1 tsp. galangal
1 tbsp. lemon grass
5 pepper corns
1 tsp. coriander root
1 tsp. kaffir lime rind
1 tsp. salt
1 tsp. shrimp paste
2 tbsp. ground dried shrimp

OTHER INGREDIENTS :

300 grams pork
200 grams yard-long beans
2 tbsp. cooking oil
1 tbsp. palm sugar
1 tbsp. fish sauce
3 kaffir lime leaves, chopped

PREPARATION :

1. Place chilli paste ingredients in mortar and pound until thoroughly ground and mixed.
2. Wash pork, cut into long, thin slices, and marinate in 1 tsp. fish sauce.
3. Wash yard-leng beans, cut into 1 inch lengths, boil until just cooked, and remove from water.
4. Heat oil in a frying pan, fry the pork until done, then remove the pork from the pan and set aside.
5. Put the chilli paste in the pan and fry until fragrant, then add the pork, sugar, fish sauce, and yard-long beans. Stir to mix. When done, scoop up onto serving plate. Top with kaffir lime leaves.

5 Serving

เครื่องปรุงน้ำพริก

พริกแห้ง 3 เม็ด หัวหอม 7 หัว
กระเทียม 2 หัว
ข่า 1 ช้อนชา ตะไคร้ 1 ช้อนโต๊ะ
พริกไทย 5 เม็ด รากผักชี 1 ช้อนชา
ผิวมะกรูด 1 ช้อนชา เกลือ 1 ช้อนชา
กะปิ 1 ช้อนชา กุ้งแห้งป่น 2 ช้อนโต๊ะ

เครื่องปรุง

เนื้อหมู 300 กรัม
ถั่วฝักยาว 200 กรัม
น้ำมัน 2 ช้อนโต๊ะ
น้ำตาลปีบ 1 ช้อนโต๊ะ น้ำปลา 1 ช้อนโต๊ะ
ใบมะกรูด หั่นฝอย 3 ใบ

วิธีทำ

1. โขลกน้ำพริกให้ละเอียด
2. ล้างเนื้อหมูหั่นชิ้นเล็ก ๆ ยาว ๆ หมักกับน้ำปลา 1 ช้อนชา
3. ล้างถั่วฝักยาว ตัดเป็นท่อนยาว 1 นิ้ว ต้มพอสุกตักขึ้น
4. ใส่น้ำมันในกระทะผัดเนื้อหมูพอสุกตักขึ้นก่อน ใส่น้ำพริกลงผัดให้หอม จึงใส่เนื้อหมูลงผัดใหม่ ใส่น้ำตาล น้ำปลา ใส่ถั่วฝักยาว ผัดพอทั่วตักขึ้น เสิร์ฟ โรยหน้าด้วยใบมะกรูด

TOM YAM KUNG
(Sour and Spicy Prawn Soup)
ต้มยำกุ้ง

INGREDIENTS :

6 large prawns, shelled and deveined

3 cups chicken stock

200 grams mushrooms, halved

1 lemon grass stem, cut into short lengths

5 slices galangal

4 tbsp. lime juice

3 tbsp. fish sauce

5-6 hot chillies, just broken with pestle

2-3 kaffir lime leaves, torn

2 coriander plants, chopped coarsely

PREPARATION :

1. Heat the stock to boiling. Add the lemon grass, galangal, prawns and mushrooms. Season to taste with lime juice, fish sauce and chillies. Add kaffir lime leaves and chopped coriander, remove from the heat, and serve hot.

2. Instead of chillies, 1 tsp. ground pepper may be mixed with the stock.

4 Serving

เครื่องปรุง

กุ้งก้ามกรามขนาดใหญ่แกะเปลือก ชักเส้นดำออก 6 ตัว

น้ำต้มกระดูกไก่ 3 ถ้วย

เห็ดล้างสะอาดผ่าครึ่ง 200 กรัม

ตะไคร้หั่นเป็นท่อนสั้น ๆ 1 ต้น

ข่าหั่นเป็นแว่น ๆ 5 แว่น

น้ำมะนาว 4 ช้อนโต๊ะ น้ำปลา 3 ช้อนโต๊ะ

พริกขี้หนูทุบพอแตก 5-6 เม็ด

ใบมะกรูดฉีกเป็นชิ้น 2-3 ใบ

ผักชีหั่นหยาบ ๆ 2 ต้น

วิธีทำ

1. ต้มน้ำกระดูกให้เดือด ใส่ตะไคร้ ข่าพอเดือด ใส่กุ้ง เห็ดทั้งให้เดือดอีกครั้ง

2. ปรุงรสด้วยน้ำมะนาว น้ำปลา พริก ใส่ใบมะกรูด ผักชี แล้วยกลงรับประทานร้อน ๆ

TOM YAM KAI
(Sour and Spicy Chicken Soup)
ต้มยำไก่

INGREDIENTS :

400 grams boneless chicken meat, diced
3 cups chicken stock
100 grams straw mushrooms, halved
6 cherry tomatoes
1 lemon grass stem cut into short lengths
2-3 kaffir lime leaves, torn
3 tbsp. fish sauce
4 tbsp. lime juice
1/2 tsp. sugar
5-6 hot chillies, just broken with pestle

PREPARATION :

Place the stock in a pot, add the lemon grass and kaffir lime leaves, and bring to a boil over medium heat. Add the chicken meat, mushroom, fish sauce, lime juice and sugar; cook slowly and uncovered for 10 minutes. Do not stir. Then add the tomatoes, and chillies and cook for 5 more minutes. Remove from heat.

4 *Serving*

เครื่องปรุง

เนื้อไก่หั่นเป็นชิ้นเล็ก 400 กรัม
น้ำต้มกระดูกไก่ 3 ถ้วย
เห็ดล้างสะอาด ผ่าครึ่ง 100 กรัม
มะเขือเทศสีดา 6 ผล
ตะไคร้หั่นเป็นท่อนสั้น ๆ 1 ต้น
ใบมะกรูดฉีกเป็นชิ้น 2-3 ใบ
น้ำปลา 3 ช้อนโต๊ะ
น้ำมะนาว 4 ช้อนโต๊ะ
น้ำตาลทราย 1/2 ช้อนชา
พริกขี้หนูทุบพอแตก 5-6 เม็ด

วิธีทำ

ต้มน้ำต้มกระดูกใช้ไฟแรงปานกลาง ใส่ตะไคร้ ใบมะกรูด พอเดือดใส่เนื้อไก่ เห็ด น้ำปลา น้ำมะนาว น้ำตาล ตั้งไฟต่อโดยไม่ต้องปิดฝาหม้อ นาน 10 นาที ไม่ต้องคน แล้วใส่มะเขือเทศและพริก ตั้งไฟต่อราว 5 นาทีจึงยกลง

KAENG LIANG
(Fish-Flavored Vegetable Soup)
แกงเลียง

INGREDIENTS FOR SPICE MIXTURE :

10 pepper corns
1 tbsp. shrimp paste
10 shallots
1/2 cup dried shrimp or fish

OTHER INGREDIENTS :

5 cups sponge gourd, bottle-gourd, straw mushrooms baby corn, and pumkin, cut into bite sizes
1 cup of sweet basil (maenglak) leaves
4 cups soup stock or water
2-3 tbsp. fish sauce

PREPARATION :

1. Place spice mixture ingredients in a mortar and pound until mixed thoroughly.
2. Add spice mixture to soup stock (or water) in a pot and heat to boiling, stirring to prevent sticking. Do not cover the pot or allow to boil over.
3. Add the vegetables and boil. When vegetables are done, season to taste with fish sauce or salt, as desired; then, remove from heat.

6 Serving

เครื่องปรุงน้ำพริก

พริกไทยเม็ด 10 เม็ด
กะปิ 1 ช้อนโต๊ะ หัวหอมแดง 10 หัว
กุ้งแห้งป่นหรือปลาแห้งป่น 1/2 ถ้วย

เครื่องปรุงอื่น ๆ

บวบ, น้ำเต้า, เห็ดฟาง, ข้าวโพดอ่อน, ฟักทอง หั่นเป็นชิ้นเล็กพอคำ 5 ถ้วย
ใบแมงลัก 1 ถ้วย
น้ำต้มกระดูกหรือน้ำเปล่า 4 ถ้วย
น้ำปลา 2-3 ช้อนโต๊ะ

วิธีทำ

1. โขลกเครื่องปรุงน้ำพริกให้ละเอียดเข้ากันดี
2. ผสมน้ำพริกกับน้ำต้มกระดูก ใส่หม้อต้มจนเดือด หมั่นคนเพื่อไม่ให้น้ำพริกจับเป็นก้อน อย่าปิดฝาหม้อหรือปล่อยให้น้ำแกงเดือดจนล้น
3. เมื่อน้ำแกงเดือดแล้วใส่ผัก พอผักสุกใส่น้ำปลา ยกลง

KUNG NEUNG SI IU
(Prawns Steamed with Soy Sauce)
กุ้งนึ่งซีอิ๊ว

INGREDIENTS :

15 prawns	
1 tbsp. chopped garlic	
2 coriander roots, chopped	
1 tbsp. light soy sauce	
1 tbsp. oyster sauce	
1/4 tsp. pepper	
1 tbsp. finely chopped spring onion	

PREPARATION :

1. Shell and devein the prawns and arrange on a plate.
2. Mix the garlic and coriander root with the soy sauce and the oyster sauce; then, pour over the prawns.
3. After the water has already begun to boil, place the prawns in the steamer. Steam about 10 minutes, remove, sprinkle with the spring onion and pepper, and serve.

4 Serving

เครื่องปรุง

กุ้งนาง 15 ตัว	
กระเทียมโขลกละเอียด 1 ช้อนโต๊ะ	
รากผักชีโขลกละเอียด 2 ราก	
ซีอิ๊วขาว 1 ช้อนโต๊ะ	
ซอสน้ำมันหอย 1 ช้อนโต๊ะ	
พริกไทย 1/4 ช้อนชา	
ต้นหอมซอย 1 ช้อนโต๊ะ	

วิธีทำ

1. ล้างกุ้งแล้วแกะเปลือก ชักเส้นดำ จัดลงจาน
2. ผสมกระเทียมและรากผักชีกับซีอิ๊วและซอสน้ำมันหอย แล้วราดลงบนตัวกุ้ง
3. ตั้งลังถึงจนน้ำเดือด แล้วใส่จานกุ้งในลังถึงนำไปนึ่งประมาณ 10 นาที ยกลง โรยด้วยพริกไทยและต้นหอมซอย

PLA KAPHONG KHAO NEUNG MANAO
(Sea Perch Steamed in Lime Sauce)

ปลากะพงขาวนึ่งมะนาว

INGREDIENTS :

1 sea perch weighing about 450 grams
3 red chillies, coarsely chopped
1 cup chicken stock
3 tbsp. lime juice
1 1/2 tbsp. light soy sauce
2 spring onions
10 peeled cloves of giant garlic

PREPARATION :

1. Scale, clean, and wash the fish. With a knife, score the flesh along the length of the fish; then, place it in a deep bowl.

2. Chop the chillies and mix them with the chicken stock, lime juice, and soy sauce. The dominant taste should be sour.

3. Pour the mixture over the fish and place the spring onions cut into lengths and the garlic alongside.

4. After the water has begun boiling, place the fish in a steamer and steam over high heat for about 15 minutes. Remove from the steamer and serve hot.

2-3 Serving

เครื่องปรุง

ปลากะพงขาวน้ำหนักประมาณ 450 กรัม 1 ตัว
พริกขี้หนู 3 เม็ด
น้ำต้มกระดูกไก่ 1 ถ้วย
น้ำมะนาว 3 ช้อนโต๊ะ
ซีอิ๊วขาว 1 1/2 ช้อนโต๊ะ
ต้นหอมตัดเป็นท่อนยาว 2 ต้น
กระเทียมกลีบใหญ่ ปอกเปลือก 10 กลีบ

วิธีทำ

1. ขอดเกล็ดปลา ควักไส้และล้างให้สะอาด ซับน้ำบั้งปลา แล้วใส่ลงใน ชามก้นลึก

2. สับพริกผสมกับน้ำต้มกระดูกไก่ เติมน้ำมะนาว ซีอิ๊ว ควรให้รสเปรี้ยวนำ

3. นำมาราดบนตัวปลา วางต้นหอมและกระเทียมไว้ข้าง ๆ

4. เมื่อน้ำเดือดเอาปลาใส่ลังถึงนึ่งนานประมาณ 15 นาที ใช้ไฟแรง ยกลง เสิร์ฟร้อน ๆ

KHAI TUN
(Beaten Egg Steamed with Pork)
ไข่ตุ๋น

INGREDIENTS :

2 eggs
1 tbsp. thinly sliced shallot
1 cup chicken stock
1/4 tsp. pepper
2 tbsp. light soy sauce
1/4 tsp. salt
3 prawns, shelled and deveined
3 tbsp. ground pork
1 coriander green

PREPARATION :

1. Beat the eggs in a mixing bowl, add the shallot, then add the stock. Add the pepper, light soy sauce and salt, stirring with a fork.

2. Divide the mixture into 3 portions. Put each portion in a small glass bowl.

3. Wrap each prawn with 1/3 of the pork.

4. After the water has begun boiling, place the cups in a steamer and steam until the egg mixture begin to cook. Place a prawn on top of the mixture in each cup. Continue steaming for about 15 minutes until the pork and prawns are done.

5. Remove the cups from the steamer and sprinkle with chopped spring onion. Serve hot.

3 Serving

เครื่องปรุง

ไข่ไก่ 2 ฟอง
หอมแดงซอย 1 ช้อนโต๊ะ
น้ำต้มกระดูกไก่ 1 ถ้วย
พริกไทยป่น 1/4 ช้อนชา
ซีอิ๊วขาว 2 ช้อนโต๊ะ เกลือ 1/4 ช้อนชา
กุ้งปอกเปลือกชักเส้นดำ 3 ตัว
หมูสับ 3 ช้อนโต๊ะ
ผักชี 1 ต้น

วิธีทำ

๑. ตีไข่ในชาม ใส่หัวหอม เติมน้ำต้มกระดูกไก่ ใส่พริกไทย ซีอิ๊ว และเกลือ คนให้เข้ากัน

๒. เทไข่ผสมใส่ถ้วยสำหรับนึ่ง 3 ถ้วย แล้วใส่ในลังถึงนึ่งขณะที่น้ำเดือด

๓. แบ่งหมูสับเป็น 3 ส่วน เอามาแผ่ห่อกุ้งแต่ละตัว

๔. เมื่อไข่เริ่มสุก วางกุ้งลงข้างบนไข่ตุ๋น ถ้วยละ 1 ตัว นึ่งต่อไปจนกุ้งและหมูสุก ประมาณ 15 นาที

๕. ยกลง โรยด้วยผักชี เสิร์ฟร้อน ๆ

KAENG KHIAO WAN NEUA
(Thai Beef Green Curry)
แกงเขียวหวานเนื้อ

INGREDIENTS :

400 grams beef
3 tbsp. green curry paste (See p.23)
400 grams grated coconut or 2 1/2 cups coconut milk
1 tbsp. cooking oil
2 kaffir lime leaves
1 1/2-2 tbsp. fish sauce
1 1/2 tsp. palm sugar
150 grams eggplant cut into bite sized pieces
1/4 cup sweet basil leaves (horapha)
2-3 red chillies cut into strips

PREPARATION :

1. Cut beef into long, thin slices.
2. Add 2 cups warm water to the coconut and squeeze out 1 cup coconut cream and 1 1/2 cups coconut milk.
3. Fry the curry paste in oil until fragrant, reduce heat, add the coconut cream a little at a time, stirring until the coconut cream begins to have an oily sheen.
4. Add the beef and torn kaffir lime leaves and cook a short time; then, pour the curry into a pot, add the coconut milk and sugar. Add fish sauce to taste, and heat. When boiling, add the eggplant. When the meat is done, add the sweet basil and chillies and remove from heat.

4 Serving

เครื่องปรุง

เนื้อวัว 400 กรัม
น้ำพริกแกงเขียวหวาน (ดูหน้า 23) 3 ช้อนโต๊ะ
มะพร้าวขูด (น้ำกะทิ 2 1/2 ถ้วย) 400 กรัม
น้ำมันพืช 1 ช้อนโต๊ะ
ใบมะกรูด 2 ใบ ฉีกเป็นชิ้นๆ
น้ำปลา 1 1/2-2 ช้อนโต๊ะ น้ำตาลปีบ 1 1/2 ช้อนชา
มะเขือ 150 กรัม ใบโหระพา 1/4 ถ้วย
พริกชี้ฟ้าแดงหั่นแฉลบ 2-3 เม็ด

วิธีทำ

1. หั่นเนื้อตามขวางเป็นชิ้นยาว บาง
2. คั้นกะทิ ใช้น้ำอุ่น 2 ถ้วย แยกหัวกะทิไว้ 1 ถ้วย หางกะทิ 1 1/2 ถ้วย
3. ผัดน้ำพริกกับน้ำมันจนหอม ลดไฟ ใส่หัวกะทิลงทีละน้อยคนให้เข้ากับน้ำพริก จนกะทิแตกมัน
4. ใส่เนื้อวัวกับใบมะกรูด สักครู่จึงตักใส่หม้อตั้งไฟ แล้วเติมหางกะทิ ปรุงรสด้วยน้ำปลาและน้ำตาลปีบ พอเดือด ใส่มะเขือ พอมะเขือสุก ใส่ใบโหระพาและพริกชี้ฟ้าแดงแล้วยกลง

PHA-NAENG NEUA
(Beef Curried in Sweet Peanut Sauce)
พะแนงเนื้อ

INGREDIENTS :

400 grams beef, cut into thin strips
2 cups coconut milk
3 tbsp. pha-naeng curry paste (or red curry paste) (See p. 22)
1/2 cup ground roasted peanuts
2 1/2 tbsp. fish sauce
1/4 tsp. salt
3 tbsp. palm sugar
6 fresh or dry kaffir lime leaves
1 red chilli thinly sliced.

PREPARATION :

1. Put 1 cup coconut milk over medium heat until some of the oil surfaces, add the curry paste and slowly bring to a boil, stirring constantly.

2. Put in beef strips and cook for 5 minutes, add 1 cup coconut milk.

3. Meanwhile, in a bowl, mix the rest of the ingredients except for the kaffir lime leaves. Add this to the curried beef, stir well and simmer about 15 minutes. Add the kaffir lime leaves and remove from the heat.

4-5 *Serving*

เครื่องปรุง

เนื้อวัวหั่นเป็นชิ้นยาว บาง 400 กรัม
กะทิ 2 ถ้วย
น้ำพริกแกงพะแนงหรือแกงแดง (ดูหน้า 22) 3 ช้อนโต๊ะ
ถั่วลิสงคั่วป่น 1/2 ถ้วย
น้ำปลา 2 1/2 ช้อนโต๊ะ เกลือ 1/4 ช้อนชา
น้ำตาลปีบ 3 ช้อนโต๊ะ
ใบมะกรูด 6 ใบ

วิธีทำ

1. ตั้งกะทิ 1 ถ้วยบนไฟปานกลาง เคี่ยวจนแตกมันใส่น้ำพริกหมั่นคน ตั้งเคี่ยวจนเป็นสีแดง

2. ใส่เนื้อวัวตั้งไฟต่อ 5 นาที จึงใส่กะทิที่เหลือ

3. ผสมเครื่องปรุงอื่น ๆ ที่เหลือ ยกเว้นใบมะกรูด ลงในหม้อ คนให้เข้ากัน เคี่ยวต่ออีก 15 นาที ใส่ใบมะกรูด แล้วยกลง

PIK KAI SOT SAI PHA-NAENG
(Stuffed Chicken Wings in Pha-naeng Sauce)

ปีกไก่สอดไส้พะแนง

INGREDIENTS :

10 chicken wings
1 cup chopped chicken breast
3 tbsp. red curry paste (See p.22)
3 cups coconut milk
3 tbsp. fish sauce
2 tbsp. palm sugar
2 tbsp. shredded kaffir lime leaves
2 red chillies, thinly sliced
1/2 cup sweet basil leaves

PREPARATION :

1. Slit open the wings, remove the bones, being careful not to tear the skin, and cut off the pointed tip of each wing.

2. Blend the chicken breast with 1 tbsp. of the red curry paste and 1 tbsp. fish sauce.

3. Put some of the stuffing into each wing but do not pack too tightly.

4. Close the slit by pinning the skin on either side together with a sliver of bamboo and shape so they look like chicken wings. Then, place the wings in a steamer and steam about 10 minutes or until done.

5. Place 1 cup of coconut milk in a wok over a medium heat. When some oil has surfaced, add the remaining red curry paste and stir to disperse. When fragrant, add the remaining coconut milk a little at a time and season with fish sauce and sugar. Now, add the steamed chicken wings, cooked 5 minutes, transfer the wings and sauce to a pot, close the lid, and simmer over a very low heat until the wings are tender and the liquid is much reduced in volume.

6. Place the wings in a serving dish and garnish with the kaffir lime leaves, chilli and sweet basil.

5 Serving

เครื่องปรุง

ปีกไก่ 10 ปีก
เนื้ออกไก่สับละเอียด 1 ถ้วย
น้ำพริกแกงแดง ดูหน้า 22) 3 ช้อนโต๊ะ
กะทิ 3 ถ้วย น้ำปลา 3 ช้อนโต๊ะ
น้ำตาลปีบ 2 ช้อนโต๊ะ
ใบมะกรูดหั่นฝอย 2 ช้อนโต๊ะ
พริกแดงหั่นแฉลบ 2 เม็ด
ใบโหระพา 1/2 ถ้วย

วิธีทำ

1. เลาะปีกไก่ เอากระดูกออก ระวังอย่าให้หนังขาด ตัดปลายปีกทิ้ง

2. ผสมเนื้อไก่สับกับน้ำพริก 1 ช้อนโต๊ะ เติมน้ำปลา 1 ช้อนโต๊ะ

3. ยัดไส้ปีกไก่ด้วยส่วนผสมเนื้อไก่กับน้ำพริก อย่าให้แน่นนัก

4. ปิดปลายด้วยไม้กลัด แต่งรูปร่างปีกไก่ที่ยัดไส้แล้วให้คืนลักษณะปีกไก่ แล้วนำไปนึ่งให้สุก (10 นาที)

5. เคี่ยวกะทิ 1 ถ้วย ไฟปานกลาง จนแตกมัน ใส่น้ำพริกแกงที่เหลือ คนให้ละลาย เติมกะทิลงไปที่ละน้อยจนหมด ปรุงรสด้วยน้ำปลา น้ำตาล ใส่ปีกไก่นึ่งลงไป พักไว้สัก 5 นาที ตักใส่หม้อปิดฝา เคี่ยวไฟอ่อนจนปีกไก่ สุกนุ่มและน้ำแกงงวดพอลูกขลิก

6. ตักปีกไก่เรียงในจาน แต่งด้วยใบมะกรูด พริกแดง และโหระพา

CHUCHI PLA THU SOT
(Fish Curry)
ฉู่ฉี่ปลาทูสด

INGREDIENTS :

400 grams mackerel or other meaty fish
2 tbsp. red curry paste (See p. 22)
3 cups coconut milk
3 tbsp. fish sauce
2 tbsp. palm sugar
2 shredded kaffir lime leaves
1/2 cup sweet basil leaves (horapha)
3 spur chillies, sliced

PREPARATION :

1. Wash and clean the fish, remove the head, and score diagonally on both sides.

2. Heat 1 cup coconut milk in a wok until some of the oil surfaces, add the curry paste and cook with stirring until dispersed and fragrant; then, add the rest of the coconut milk and, when it comes to a boil, add the fish. Simmer for 15 minutes until the fish is done.

3. Season to taste with fish sauce and palm sugar.

4. Dip onto a serving platter and garnish with shreds of kaffir lime leaves, sweet basil leaves and chillies.

3 Serving

เครื่องปรุง

ปลาทูสดหรือปลาชนิดอื่น 400 กรัม
น้ำพริกแกงแดง (ดูหน้า 22) 2 ช้อนโต๊ะ
กะทิ 3 ถ้วย
น้ำปลา 3 ช้อนโต๊ะ
น้ำตาลปีบ 2 ช้อนโต๊ะ
ใบมะกรูดหั่นฝอย 2 ใบ
ใบโหระพา 1/2 ถ้วย
พริกชี้ฟ้าแดง (หั่นแฉลบหรือจักเป็นดอก) 3 เม็ด

วิธีทำ

1. ล้างปลาให้สะอาด ตัดหัว ควักไส้ ตัดครึ่งตัว บั้งทั้งสองด้าน

2. เคี่ยวกะทิ 1 ถ้วยจนแตกมัน ใส่น้ำพริกผัดจนหอม เติมกะทิลงไปจนหมด เมื่อน้ำแกงเดือด ใส่ปลาลงไป ตั้งไฟต่อสัก 15 นาที จนสุก

3. ปรุงรสด้วยน้ำปลา และน้ำตาล

4. ตักใส่จาน แต่งด้วยใบมะกรูดหั่นฝอย ใบโหระพาและพริกชี้ฟ้าแดง

KAENG PHET PET YANG
(Red Curry of Duck)
แกงเผ็ดเป็ดย่าง

INGREDIENTS :

1 roasted duck, deboned and cut into 1 inch strips
3 tbsp. red curry paste (See p.22)
1 1/2 tbsp. vegetable oil
2 1/2 cups coconut milk
1/2 cup water (or chicken stock)
10 cherry tomatoes, (or 2 medium tomatoes halved)
1 cup eggplant (makheua phuang)
4 kaffir lime leaves, halved
2 tbsp. fish sauce
1/2 tsp. salt
1 tsp. sugar

PREPARATION :

1. Put vegetable oil into wok over medium heat and add the red curry paste, stir well, add 3/4 cups coconut milk and stir to mix thoroughly.

2. Add the duck and stir well. Next pour the mixture into a pot, add the remaining coconut milk, water, tomatoes, eggplants, kaffir lime leaves, sugar, salt and fish sauce. Bring to a boil and remove from heat.

4 Serving

เครื่องปรุง

เป็ดย่างถอดกระดูกออก หั่นเป็นชิ้นขนาด 1 นิ้ว 1 ตัว
น้ำพริกแกงแดง (ดูหน้า 22) 3 ช้อนโต๊ะ
น้ำมันพืช 1 1/2 ช้อนโต๊ะ กะทิ 2 1/2 ถ้วย
น้ำต้มกระดูกไก่หรือน้ำเปล่า 1/2 ถ้วย
มะเขือเทศสีดา (หรือมะเขือเทศขนาดกลางผ่าครึ่ง 2 ผล) 10 ผล
มะเขือพวง 1 ถ้วย
ใบมะกรูดฉีก 4 ใบ
น้ำปลา 2 ช้อนโต๊ะ เกลือ 1/2 ช้อนชา
น้ำตาล 1 ช้อนชา

วิธีทำ

1. ผัดน้ำพริกกับน้ำมัน ใช้ไฟกลาง จนหอมใส่กะทิ 3/4 ถ้วย คนให้เข้ากัน

2. ใส่เนื้อเป็ดลงไปผัด คักส่วนผสมลงหม้อ เติมกะทิ น้ำต้มกระดูกไก่ ใส่มะเขือเทศ มะเขือพวง ใบมะกรูด ปรุงรสด้วยน้ำปลา น้ำตาล เกลือ ตั้งไฟต่อจนเดือด แล้วยกลง

KAENG PHET KAI SAI NO MAI
(Chicken in Red Curry with Bamboo Shoots)
แกงเผ็ดไก่ใส่หน่อไม้

INGREDIENTS :

400 grams diced, boneless chicken
1 tbsp. red curry paste (See p.22)
2 cups coconut milk
300 grams bamboo shoots (sliced lengthwise)
2 tbsp. fish sauce
1/4 tsp. salt
1 1/2 tsp. sugar
5 kaffir lime leaves, halved
1 fresh red chilli (sliced lengthwise into 8 pieces)
1/2 cups sweet basil leaves (horapha)

PREPARATION :

1. In a pot, bring half the coconut milk to a slow boil, stirring constantly. Put in the red curry paste and chicken, stir well, and cook until done (about 5 minutes).

2. Add the remaining coconut milk, bamboo shoots, sugar and fish sauce, and bring slowly to a boil. Add salt to taste.

3. Add kaffir lime leaves, and chilli, and remove from heat. Garnish with sweet basil.

4 Serving

เครื่องปรุง

เนื้อไก่ หั่นเป็นชิ้นเล็ก ๆ 400 กรัม
เครื่องแกงเผ็ด 1 ช้อนโต๊ะ (ดูหน้า 22)
กะทิ 2 ถ้วย
หน่อไม้หั่นเป็นชิ้นเล็กๆ ยาวๆ 300 กรัม
น้ำปลา 2 ช้อนโต๊ะ เกลือ 1/4 ช้อนชา
น้ำตาล 1 1/2 ช้อนชา ใบมะกรูดฉีกเป็นชิ้น 5 ใบ
พริกชี้ฟ้าแดงหั่นเป็นชิ้นเล็กยาว 1 เม็ด
ใบโหระพา 1/2 ถ้วย

วิธีทำ

1. ใส่กะทิครึ่งหนึ่งลงในหม้อ ตั้งไฟปานกลางหมั่นคนจนเดือด ใส่น้ำพริก
ลงคนให้เข้ากันดี แล้วใส่ไก่ ต้ม 5 นาทีหรือจนไก่สุก

2. เติมกะทิที่เหลือลงไป ใส่หน่อไม้ ปรุงรสด้วยน้ำปลา น้ำตาล และเกลือ
พอเดือด

3. ใส่ใบมะกรูด พริก แล้วยกลง แต่งด้วยใบโหระพา

KAENG KA-RI KUNG
(Curried Prawns)
แกงกะหรี่กุ้ง

INGREDIENTS :

500 grams shelled and deveined prawns
2 1/2 cups coconut milk
1 tbsp. yellow curry paste (Nam Phrik Kaeng Ka-ri) (See p. 24)
1 tbsp. fish sauce
1/2 tsp. salt
1 1/2 tsp. sugar
1/2 cup cherry tomatoes
2 fresh chillies, deseeded and sliced

PREPARATION :

1. Put 3/4 cups of coconut milk into a wok or pan, bring to boil over midium heat, stirring constantly, and boil for 5 minutes.

2. Add the curry paste, stir well, and simmer for 10 minutes.

3. Then, add the fish sauce, sugar, salt and remaining coconut milk and simmer for 10 more minutes, stirring regularly.

4. Finally, put in the cheries tomatoes, prawns and chillies, bring to a boil, and remove from heat.

5. Serve with cucumber relish. (See p.167)

4 Serving

เครื่องปรุง

กุ้งตัวใหญ่ปอกเปลือกชักเส้นดำ 500 กรัม
กะทิ 2 1/2 ถ้วย
น้ำพริกแกงกะหรี่ (ดูหน้า 24) 1 ช้อนโต๊ะ
น้ำปลา 1 ช้อนโต๊ะ เกลือ 1/2 ช้อนชา
น้ำตาล 1 1/2 ช้อนชา
มะเขือเทศสีดา 1/2 ถ้วย
พริกชี้ฟ้าหั่นเป็นชิ้นยาวๆ บางๆ 2 เม็ด

วิธีทำ

1. ใส่กะทิ 3/4 ถ้วยในกระทะ ตั้งไฟปานกลาง หมั่นคน ทิ้งให้เดือด นาน 5 นาที

2. ใส่น้ำพริกลงไป คนให้ละลาย เคี่ยวประมาณ 10 นาที

3. ปรุงรสด้วยน้ำปลา น้ำตาล เกลือ ใส่กะทิที่เหลือลงไป เคี่ยวอีก 10 นาที หมั่นคน

4. ใส่มะเขือเทศ กุ้ง และพริก เมื่อเดือดยกลง เสิร์ฟกับอาจาด

HO MOK PLA REU KAI REU MU
(Steamed Curried Fish, Chicken, or Pork)
ห่อหมกปลาหรือไก่ หรือหมู

INGREDIENTS FOR SPICE MIXTURE :

5 dried chillies, seeds removed and soaked in water
3 garlic bulbs
2 tbsp. finely sliced galangal
1 tsp. finely sliced kaffir-lime rind
2 tsp. finely sliced coriander root
5 pepper corns
1/2 tsp. salt
1 tsp. shrimp paste
1 tsp. finely sliced krachai (if fish is used)

OTHER INGREDIENTS :

400 grams filleted fish, chicken, or pork
2 cups coconut milk
1 tsp. rice flour
1 egg
3 tbsp. fish sauce
2 cups sweet basil leaves (horapha)
2 tbsp. finely chopped coriander greens
3 tbsp. shredded kaffir-lime leaves
1 finely sliced red chilli

PREPARATION :

1. Pound the spice mixture ingredients well in a mortar.
2. Cut the fish fillets into thin slices; if chicken is used, cut it into small pieces; if pork is used, chop it but not too finely.
3. Skim 3/4 cup coconut cream from the coconut milk, add rice flour, bring to a boil, remove from the heat, and set aside for topping.
4. Stir 1 cup coconut milk with the pounded spice mixture, add the fish or meat, the egg, the fish sauce, and then the remaining coconut milk a little at a time. Add 1/2 cup basil leaves, 1 tbsp. coriander greens, and 2 tsp. kaffir lime leaf and stir to mix in.
5. Place the remaining sweet basil leaves in the bottoms of custard cups, fill each cup with the spice mixture, and steam for 15 minutes. Remove the cups from the steamer, top each one with some of the boiled coconut cream and a little coriander greens, kaffir lime leaf, and sliced chilli. Return to the steamer to steam for one minute, and then remove from the steamer. Shredded cabbage may be substituted for sweet basil leaves.

6 Serving

เครื่องปรุงน้ำพริก

พริกแห้ง เอาเมล็ดออก แช่น้ำ 5 เม็ด
กระเทียม 3 หัว ข่าซอยละเอียด 2 ช้อนโต๊ะ
ตะไคร้ซอยละเอียด 2 ช้อนโต๊ะ
ผิวมะกรูดซอยละเอียด 1 ช้อนชา
รากผักชีหั่นละเอียด 2 ช้อนชา พริกไทย 5 เม็ด
เกลือ 1/2 ช้อนชา กะปิ 1 ช้อนชา
ใช้เนื้อปลาเพิ่มกระชายหั่นละเอียด 1 ช้อนชา

เครื่องปรุงอื่น ๆ

เนื้อปลา เนื้อไก่ หรือเนื้อหมู 400 กรัม
กะทิ 2 ถ้วย แป้งข้าวเจ้า 1 ช้อนชา ไข่ 1 ฟอง
น้ำปลา 3 ช้อนโต๊ะ ใบโหระพา 2 ถ้วย
ผักชีหั่นละเอียด 2 ช้อนโต๊ะ ใบมะกรูดหั่นฝอย 3 ช้อนโต๊ะ
พริกชี้ฟ้าแดงซอยละเอียด 1 เม็ด

วิธีทำ

1. โขลกหรือปั่นเครื่องปรุงน้ำพริกให้ละเอียดเข้ากันดี
2. เนื้อปลาแล่เป็นชิ้นบาง ๆ ถ้าเนื้อไก่หั่นเป็นชิ้นเล็ก ๆ ถ้าเนื้อหมูสับหยาบ ๆ
3. ช้อนหัวกะทิขึ้นไว้ 3/4 ถ้วย ใส่แป้งข้าวเจ้าลงในหัวกะทิคนให้ละลาย แล้วต้มจนเดือด ยกลงพักไว้ใช้ราดหน้าห่อหมก
4. แบ่งกะทิมา 1 ถ้วย คนกับน้ำพริกจนละลายเข้ากันดี ใส่ปลาหรือไก่ หรือหมูลงไป ใส่ไข่ น้ำปลา ลงไปคน ค่อย ๆ เติมกะทิที่เหลือลงไปคนด้วย ทีละน้อย ใส่ใบโหระพา 1/2 ถ้วย ผักชี 1 ช้อนโต๊ะ และใบมะกรูด 2 ช้อนชา ลงไปคนให้เข้ากัน
5. รองก้นถ้วยด้วยใบโหระพา ตักส่วนผสมใส่ลงไป จัดเรียงลงลังถึงนึ่ง ประมาณ 15 นาที ยกลงราดหน้าห่อหมกด้วยหัวกะทิที่เตรียมไว้ โรยหน้า ด้วยผักชี ใบมะกรูด และพริกชี้ฟ้า เอาขึ้นนึ่งต่ออีก 1 นาที แล้วยกลง อาจใช้กะหล่ำปลีหั่นฝอยแทนใบโหระพาก็ได้

KAENG PHET HET
(Red Curry of Mushrooms)
แกงเผ็ดเห็ด

INGREDIENTS :

1 1/2 cups coconut milk
1 tbsp. red curry paste (See p. 22)
1/2 cup water (or chicken stock)
300 grams fresh mushrooms (halved)
3 tbsp. fish sauce
1/2 tbsp. sugar
3-4 fresh kaffir lime leaves, torn
1 sliced whole medium red or green chilli

PREPARATION :

1. Put half of the coconut milk in a wok over medium heat until boiled and some of the oil surface. Add the red curry paste and stir until thoroughly mixed.
2. Add the remaining coconut milk, chicken stock, mushrooms, fish sauce, sugar, kaffir lime leaves, and chilli. Do not overcook the mushrooms.

3 Serving

เครื่องปรุง

กะทิ 1 1/2 ถ้วย
น้ำพริกแกงแดง (ดูหน้า 22) 1 ช้อนโต๊ะ
น้ำต้มกระดูกไก่ หรือน้ำเปล่า 1/2 ถ้วย
เห็ดสด ล้าง ผ่าครึ่ง 300 กรัม
น้ำปลา 3 ช้อนโต๊ะ
น้ำตาล 1/2 ช้อนโต๊ะ
ใบมะกรูดฉีก 3-4 ใบ
พริกชี้ฟ้าเขียวหรือแดงหั่นฝอย 1 เม็ด

วิธีทำ

1. แบ่งกะทิใส่ลงกระทะครึ่งหนึ่ง ตั้งไฟปานกลาง ผัดพอกะทิแตกมัน ใส่น้ำพริกลงผัดจนเข้ากันดี
2. เติมกะทิที่เหลือลงไป แล้วใส่น้ำต้มกระดูกไก่ เห็ด ปรุงรสด้วยน้ำปลา น้ำตาล ใส่ใบมะกรูด และพริก ระวังอย่าให้เห็ดสุกจนเกินไป

YAM THUA PHU
(Spicy Winged-Bean Salad)
ยำถั่วพู

INGREDIENTS :

300 grams winged beans

1/2 cup steamed pork sliced into small pieces

1/2 cup coconut milk

2 tbsp. fried sliced shallot

2 tbsp. coarsely ground roasted peanuts

2 tbsp. fish sauce

1 1/2 tbsp. sugar

2 tbsp. lime juice

2 small pan-roasted dried chillies,

2 small roasted shallots

1 small roasted garlic bulb

5-7 fried dried hot chillies

1 lettuce plant

PREPARATION :

1. Immerse the winged beans in boiling water for 3 minutes and put in cool water, then cut into small pieces.

2. Bring the coconut milk to a boil and then remove from the heat. Divide into 2 equal portions.

3. Pound chilli, the roasted shallots, and the garlic well in a mortar ; then add the sugar, fish sauce, and lime juice, stir to mix thoroughly, and transfer to a bowl.

4. Add the winged beans, pork, half of the boiled coconut milk, fried shallot, and peanut, toss to mix well, and then place on a bed of lettuce. Pour the rest of boiled coconut milk on the mixture. Serve with fried dried chillies.

4 Serving

เครื่องปรุง

ถั่วพู 300 กรัม

เนื้อหมูนึ่งหรือต้มสุกหั่นเป็นชิ้นเล็ก 1/2 ถ้วย

กะทิ 1/2 ถ้วย

หอมแดงซอยแล้วเจียว 2 ช้อนโต๊ะ

ถั่วลิสงคั่วบด 2 ช้อนโต๊ะ น้ำปลา 2 ช้อนโต๊ะ

น้ำตาล 1 1/2 ช้อนโต๊ะ น้ำมะนาว 2 ช้อนโต๊ะ

พริกขี้หนูแห้งคั่ว 2 เม็ด

หอมแดงเผา 2 หัว

กระเทียมเผา 1 หัว

พริกทอด 5-7 เม็ด ผักกาดหอม 1 ต้น

วิธีทำ

1. ลวกถั่วพูในน้ำเดือด ราว 3 นาที ตักขึ้นแช่น้ำเย็นแล้วหั่นเป็นชิ้นเล็ก ๆ

2. ใส่กะทิในหม้อ ตั้งไฟจนเดือดแล้วยกลง แบ่งออกเป็น 2 ส่วน

3. โขลกพริก หอมแดง และกระเทียมให้แหลก แล้วเติมน้ำตาล น้ำปลา น้ำมะนาว คนให้น้ำตาลละลายเข้ากันดี ตักใส่ชามผสมอาหาร

4. ใส่ถั่วพู เนื้อหมู กะทิ 1 ส่วน หอมเจียว ถั่ว ลงในชามผสม คลุกให้เข้ากันดีกับน้ำปรุงรส แล้วตักใส่จาน เสิร์ฟกับพริกทอดและผักกาดหอม

YAM SAM SAHAI
(Spicy Pork, Prawn, and Chicken Salad)
ยำสามสหาย

INGREDIENTS :

1 1/2 cups slices of steamed pork
1 1/2 cups slices of steamed chicken
1 1/2 cups slices of steamed prawn
(In each case, the slices should be cut on a diagonal to the grain of the meat.)
3 tbsp. roasted chilli paste (nam phrik phao) (See p.)
3 tbsp. fish sauce
1 tsp. sugar
2-3 tbsp. tamarind juice
1/4 cup lime juice
1/4 cup roasted cashew nuts or peanuts, broken into chunks
1 lettuce plant
1/2 head cabbage, chopped
1 carrot, chopped

PREPARATION :

1. Make the sauce by mixing the roasted chilli paste, fish sauce, sugar, and tamarind juice in a pot and heating to a boil. Allow to boil a few moments ; then, remove from the heat, add the lime juice, and stir.

2. When the sauce has cooled, add the pork, chicken, and prawn ; stir to mix thoroughly. Scoop onto a platter, sprinkle with peanuts or cashews and serve with lettuce, carrot and cabbage.

4 Serving

เครื่องปรุง

เนื้อหมูต้มหรือนึ่งสุกหั่นเป็นชิ้นบาง 1 1/2 ถ้วย
เนื้อไก่ต้มหรือนึ่งสุกหั่นเป็นชิ้นบาง 1 1/2 ถ้วย
กุ้งขนาดกลางต้มหรือนึ่งสุกหั่นเป็นชิ้นบาง 1 1/2 ถ้วย
น้ำพริกเผา 3 ช้อนโต๊ะ น้ำปลา 3 ช้อนโต๊ะ
น้ำตาลทราย 1 ช้อนชา น้ำส้มมะขาม 2-3 ช้อนโต๊ะ
น้ำมะนาว 1/4 ถ้วย
ถั่วลิสงหรือเม็ดมะม่วงหิมพานต์คั่วโขลกหยาบ ๆ 1/4 ถ้วย
ผักกาดหอม 1 ต้น
กะหล่ำปลีหั่นฝอย 1/2 หัว
แครอทหั่นฝอย 1 หัว

วิธีทำ

1. ทำน้ำปรุงรสโดยผสมน้ำพริกเผากับน้ำปลา น้ำตาล น้ำส้มมะขามในหม้อ ตั้งไฟจนเดือด ทิ้งให้เดือดสักครู่หนึ่งจึงยกลง เติมน้ำมะนาว คนให้เข้ากัน

2. เมื่อน้ำปรุงรสเย็นแล้ว ใส่หมู ไก่และกุ้ง ลงไปคลุกให้เข้ากัน แล้วตัก ใส่จานเสิร์ฟ โรยถั่วลิสงหรือเม็ดมะม่วงหิมพานต์ เสิร์ฟกับผักกาดหอม และ กะหล่ำปลีกับแครอทหั่นฝอย

SALAT KHAEK
(Southern Thai Salad)
สลัดแขก

INGREDIENTS FOR DRESSING :

2 dried chillies, seeds removed and soaked in water
1/4 tsp. salt
1/4 cup thinly sliced shallot
1 tsp. curry powder
1/2 cup ground roasted peanuts
2 hard-boiled eggs
2 cups coconut milk
3 tbsp. fish sauce
1/3 cup sugar
1/4 cup tamarind juice

PREPARATION :

1. Pound the chillies, salt, shallot, and curry powder well in a mortar and then mix in the peanut. Remove the yolks from the two eggs and mix the yolks into the chilli paste.

2. Heat 1 cup of the coconut milk. When some oil has surfaced, add the chilli paste, stir to disperse, and cook until fragrant; then, add the remaining coconut milk and fish sauce, sugar, and tamarind juice.

INGREDIENTS FOR SALAD :

1 potato, peeled
3 hard-boiled eggs cuts into slices
1 cake firm white beancurd
1 lettuce plant
1 cup scalded bean sprouts
5 cucumbers
1 onion
2 tomatoes
2 cups cooking oil

PREPARATION :

1. Cut the potato into very thin slices, soak in water, drain well, and then fry in the hot oil until crisp and golden brown.Cut the beancurd into thin slices and fry in the oil until crisps.

2. Cut the cucumbers, onion and the tomatoes into thin slices.

3. Arrange the lettuce on a platter, add the cucumbers, bean sprouts, onion, tomatoes, egg, beancurd, and potato, spoon on the salad dressing, and serve right away.

4 Serving

เครื่องปรุงน้ำสลัด

พริกแห้ง แกะเมล็ดออก แช่น้ำ 2 เม็ด
เกลือ 1/4 ช้อนชา หอมแดงซอย 1/4 ถ้วย
ผงกะหรี่ 1 ช้อนชา ถั่วลิสงคั่วบด 1/2 ถ้วย
ไข่ไก่ต้มสุก 2 ฟอง กะทิ 2 ถ้วย
น้ำปลา 3 ช้อนโต๊ะ น้ำตาลทราย 1/3 ถ้วย
น้ำส้มมะขาม 1/4 ถ้วย

วิธีทำ

1. โขลกพริก เกลือ หัวหอม และผงกะหรี่ให้แหลกเข้ากัน แล้วใส่ถั่วกับไข่แดงลงผสม

2. แบ่งกะทิ 1 ถ้วยตั้งไฟ พอกะทิเริ่มแตกมันใส่น้ำพริกลงผัดจนส่งกลิ่นหอม แล้วจึงใส่กะทิที่เหลือ ปรุงรสด้วยน้ำปลา น้ำตาลและน้ำส้มมะขาม

เครื่องปรุงสลัด

มันฝรั่ง 1 ลูก
ไข่ไก่ต้มสุกหั่นเป็นชิ้นยาว 3 ฟอง
เต้าหู้ขาวชนิดแข็ง 1 ก้อน
ผักกาดหอม 1 ต้น ถั่วงอกลวก 1 ถ้วย
แตงกวา 5 ผล หอมใหญ่ 1 หัว
มะเขือเทศ 2 ผล น้ำมันพืช 2 ถ้วย

วิธีทำ

1. ปอกเปลือกมันฝรั่งหั่นเป็นแผ่นบาง ๆ แช่น้ำ แล้วพักให้สะเด็ดน้ำ ก่อนนำลงทอดในน้ำมันร้อนจัดจนเหลือง กรอบดี หั่นเต้าหู้เป็นชิ้นบาง ทอดให้เหลือง กรอบ ตักขึ้นพักให้สะเด็ดน้ำมัน

2. หั่นแตงกวา หัวหอม และมะเขือเทศตามขวางผลเป็นชิ้นบาง

3. จัดผักกาดหอมลงจาน ใส่แตงกวา ถั่วงอก หัวหอม มะเขือเทศ ไข่ เต้าหู้ และมันลงไปตามลำดับ ราดหน้าด้วยน้ำสลัด รับประทานทันที

YAM WUN SEN
(Spicy Mungbean Noodle Salad)
ยำวุ้นเส้น

INGREDIENTS FOR DRESSING :

1 tbsp. thinly sliced coriander root
1 tbs. thinly sliced bulb of pickled garlic
1 chilli
1/3 cup vinegar
1/3 cup sugar
1 tsp. salt

PREPARATION :

Pound the coriander root, pickled garlic, and chilli well in a mortar. Place this mixture in a pot, add the vinegar, sugar and salt, and heat. When the mixture comes to a boil, remove from the heat and allow to cool.

INGREDIENTS FOR SALAD :

2 cups short lengths of scalded mungbean noodles
1/2 cup thin slices of boiled pork
1/2 cup thin slices of boiled pork liver
1/2 cup thin slices of boiled prawn
1/2 cup spring onions cut into short lengths
1/2 cup 1-inch lengths of celery
1 lettuce plant
1/4 cup crisp fried dried shrimp

PREPARATION :

1. Mix the noodles, pork, liver, prawn, spring onion, and celery. Add the dressing and toss gently.
2. Place the salad on a bed of lettuce and sprinkle with the fried dried shrimp garnish with red chilli.

> 5 *Serving*

เครื่องปรุงน้ำปรุงรส

รากผักชีหั่นฝอย 1 ช้อนโต๊ะ
กระเทียมดองหั่นบาง 1 ช้อนชา
พริก 1 เม็ด น้ำส้มสายชู 1/3 ถ้วย
น้ำตาลทราย 1/3 ถ้วย เกลือ 1 ช้อนชา

วิธีทำ

โขลกรากผักชีกับกระเทียมดองและพริกพอแหลก ตักใส่หม้อใบเล็ก ใส่ น้ำส้ม น้ำตาล และเกลือ ตั้งไฟพอเดือดยกลง ทิ้งไว้ให้เย็น

เครื่องปรุงอื่น ๆ

วุ้นเส้นแช่น้ำตัดเป็นท่อนสั้นแล้วลวก 2 ถ้วย
หมูต้มสุกหั่นเป็นชิ้นบาง 1/2 ถ้วย
ตับหมูต้มสุกหั่นเป็นชิ้นบาง 1/2 ถ้วย
กุ้งต้มสุกหั่นเป็นชิ้นบาง 1/2 ถ้วย
ต้นหอมหั่นเป็นท่อนสั้น 1/2 ถ้วย
ขึ้นฉ่ายหั่นเป็นท่อนยาว 1 นิ้ว 1/2 ถ้วย
ผักกาดหอม 1 ต้น กุ้งแห้งทอดกรอบ 1/4 ถ้วย

วิธีทำ

1. ผสมวุ้นเส้น หมู ตับหมู กุ้ง ต้นหอม ขึ้นฉ่าย เข้าด้วยกัน คลุกกับ น้ำปรุงรส คลุกเบามือ
2. ตักเสิร์ฟในจานที่รองด้วยใบผักกาดหอม โรยหน้าด้วยกุ้งแห้งทอด แต่ง ด้วยพริกแดง

YAM PLA KRAPONG
(Spicy Sardine Salad)
ยำปลากระป๋อง

INGREDIENTS:

2 cans sardines
2 tbsp. shredded ginger
1/4 cup thinly sliced shallot
1 tbsp. chopped spring onion
1/4 cup mint leaves
3 tbsp. lime juice
1/4 tsp. salt
1/2 tsp. chopped hot chillies
lettuce
spring onions

PREPARATION:

1. Mix the chillies with the salt and lime juice.
2. Mix the sardines with the ginger, shallot, spring onion and mint leaves and then pour on the chilli-lime juice mixture.
3. Serve with lettuce and spring onions.

YAM KHAI TOM
(Spicy Egg Salad)
ยำไข่ต้ม

INGREDIENTS:

5 hard-boiled eggs	
1/4 cup thinly sliced shallot	
1/4 cup coarsely chopped green mango or apple	
1/4 cup mint leaves	
2 tbsp. chopped spring onion	
1 tsp. thinly sliced hot chilli	
2 tbsp. thinly sliced pickled garlic	
3 tbsp. lime juice	1 tsp. salt
lettuce	
shredded cabbage	
shredded carrot	

PREPARATION:

1. For the dressing, mix the lime juice with the pickled garlic, salt and chilli.
2. Remove the eggs from the shells and cut into slices 1/4-1/2-inch thick. Place the slices in a mixing bowl together with the shallot, mango, and spring onion and toss with the dressing; then, sprinkle with the mint leaves and arrange on a serving platter with lettuce, cabbage, and carrot.

เครื่องปรุง

ปลากระป๋อง (ปลาซาร์ดีน) 2 กระป๋อง
ขิงซอย 2 ช้อนโต๊ะ หอมแดงซอย 1/4 ถ้วย
ต้นหอมหั่นหยาบ 1 ช้อนโต๊ะ
ใบสะระแหน่ 1/4 ถ้วย น้ำมะนาว 3 ช้อนโต๊ะ
เกลือ 1/4 ช้อนชา พริกขี้หนูหั่นละเอียด 1/2 ช้อนชา
ผักกาดหอม ต้นหอม

วิธีทำ

1. ผสมพริกกับเกลือและน้ำมะนาว เป็นน้ำปรุงรส
2. เคล้าปลากระป๋องกับขิง หัวหอม ต้นหอม และใบสะระแหน่ และน้ำปรุงรส
3. ตักใส่จานเสิร์ฟที่ปูใบผักกาดหอมรองไว้ เสิร์ฟกับต้นหอม

เครื่องปรุง

ไข่ไก่ต้มสุก 5 ฟอง หอมแดงซอย 1/4 ถ้วย
มะม่วงดิบหรือแอปเปิ้ลเขียวซอยหยาบ 1/4 ถ้วย
ใบสะระแหน่ 1/4 ถ้วย ต้นหอมหั่นหยาบ 2 ช้อนโต๊ะ
พริกขี้หนูหั่นละเอียด 1 ดอก
กระเทียมดองซอยตามขวาง 2 ช้อนโต๊ะ
น้ำมะนาว 3 ช้อนโต๊ะ เกลือ 1 ช้อนชา
ผักกาดหอม กะหล่ำปลีหั่นฝอย แครอทซอยละเอียด

วิธีทำ

1. ทำน้ำปรุงรส โดยผสมน้ำมะนาวกับกระเทียมดองเกลือและพริก
2. ปอกเปลือกไข่ต้ม แล้วผ่าไข่ออกเป็นแว่น หนา 1/4-1/2 นิ้ว ใส่ไข่ลงในชามผสมอาหาร ใส่หัวหอม มะม่วง ต้นหอม ราดน้ำปรุงรส เคล้าเบา ๆ ตักใส่จานโรยหน้าด้วยใบสะระแหน่หรือผักชีเสิร์ฟกับผักกาดหอม กะหล่ำปลีและแครอท

YAM SAIKROK KAP HAEM
(Spicy Frankfurter-and-Ham Salad)
ยำไส้กรอกกับแฮม

INGREDIENTS :

150 grams frankfurters
150 grams sliced ham
100 grams roasted cashew nuts
2 tbsp. roasted chilli paste (nam phrik phao)
3 tbsp. tamarind juice
1/2 tsp. salt
1 tbsp. lime juice
1 onion sliced thin
1 lettuce

PREPARATION :

1. Cut the frankfurters diagonally into slices about 1/5-inch thick. Cut the ham into strips about 1/2-inch wide.

2. Make up the dressing by mixing the roasted chilli paste with the tamarind juice and salt, bringing the mixture to a boil, and then adding the lime juice before removing from the heat.

3. Toss the frankfurter, ham, cashews and onion together with the dressing and then spoon onto a bed of lettuce prepared on a platter. Garnish with carrots or chillies and serve with vegetables, such as Chinese cabbage and spring onions.

5-6 Serving

เครื่องปรุง

ไส้กรอก 150 กรัม
แฮมชนิดแผ่น 150 กรัม
เม็ดมะม่วงหิมพานต์ทอด 100 กรัม
น้ำพริกเผา 2 ช้อนโต๊ะ
น้ำมะขามเปียก 3 ช้อนโต๊ะ
เกลือ 1/2 ช้อนชา
น้ำมะนาว 1 ช้อนโต๊ะ
หอมหัวใหญ่ซอย 1 หัว
ผักกาดหอม 1 ต้น

วิธีทำ

1. หั่นไส้กรอกแฉลบเป็นชิ้นหนาราว 1/5 นิ้ว หั่นแฮมเป็นชิ้นยาว กว้างประมาณ 1/2 นิ้ว

2. ทำน้ำปรุงรสโดยผสมน้ำพริกเผากับน้ำมะขามเปียกและเกลือ ต้มจนเดือด เติมน้ำมะนาวแล้วยกลง

3. คลุกไส้กรอก แฮม เม็ดมะม่วงหิมพานต์และหอมหัวใหญ่กับน้ำปรุงรสให้เข้ากันดี แล้วตักใส่จานเสิร์ฟที่มีผักกาดหอมปูรอง ตกแต่งด้วยแครอทหรือพริก รับประทานกับผักเช่น ผักกาดขาว ต้นหอม

YAM KAI YANG
(Spicy Barbecued-Chicken Salad)
ยำไก่ย่าง

INGREDIENTS FOR SPICE SAUCE DRESSING :

1 tsp. ground chilli
2 tbsp. vinegar
2 tbsp. lime juice
1 tsp. sugar
2 tbsp. fish sauce
1/4 tsp. salt

OTHER INGREDIENTS :

1 barbecued chicken
1 1/2 tbsp. ground roasted peanuts
3 spring onions, cut into short lenghts
3-4 leaves lettuce

PREPARATION :

1. Make up the dressing by mixing all ingredients and then heating to a boil. Add the peanuts.
2. Separate the chicken meat into small pieces.
3. Pour the dressing onto the chicken and stir lightly. Add the spring onions and stir again.
4. Spoon the salad onto a bed of lettuce arranged on a platter, serve with fresh vegetables, such as cabbage, tomato and onion.

4 Serving

เครื่องปรุงน้ำปรุงรส

พริกบดหรือโขลก 1 ช้อนชา
น้ำส้มสายชู 2 ช้อนโต๊ะ
น้ำมะนาว 2 ช้อนโต๊ะ
น้ำตาลทราย 1 ช้อนชา
น้ำปลา 2 ช้อนโต๊ะ เกลือ 1/4 ช้อนชา

เครื่องปรุงอื่น ๆ

ไก่ย่าง 1 ตัว
ถั่วลิสงคั่วป่น 1 1/2 ช้อนโต๊ะ
ต้นหอมหั่นเป็นท่อนสั้น 3 ต้น
ผักกาดหอม 3-4 ก้าน

วิธีทำ

1. ผสมเครื่องปรุงน้ำปรุงรสทั้งหมดเข้าด้วยกันในหม้อเล็ก ๆ ตั้งไฟจนเดือด แล้วจึงใส่ถั่วป่น
2. เลาะเนื้อไก่เอากระดูกออกหั่นเป็นชิ้นบาง ๆ เล็ก
3. ราดน้ำพริกยำลงบนไก่ คลุกให้ทั่วแต่เพียงเบามือ ใส่ต้นหอม คลุกอีก ครั้งหนึ่ง
4. ตักใส่จานเสิร์ฟที่มีผักกาดหอมปูรอง รับประทานกับผักสด เช่น กะหล่ำปลี มะเขือเทศ หอมหัวใหญ่

LAP KAI
(Savory Chopped-Chicken Salad)
ลาบไก่

INGREDIENTS :

3 cups coarsely chopped chicken
1 tsp. salt
1/2 tsp. ground chilli
2 tbsp. ground pan-roasted rice or dry breadcrumbs
5 thinly sliced shallots
3 sliced spring onions
1/4 cup lime juice
1/4 cup mint leaves
2 tbsp. chopped coriander leaves

PREPARATION :

1. Mix the chicken and the salt, place in a covered baking dish, and bake at 400°F for about ten minutes until done. After removing from the oven and allowing to cool somewhat, knead to break up the mass of baked chicken.

2. Add the ground chilli, pan-roasted rice (or breadcrumbs), shallots, spring onions, and lime juice; toss gently. Add the mint leaves and coriander greens, toss once again, spoon in platter; serve with lettuce, Chinese cabbage, cucumber, yard-long beans, and spring onions.

4 Serving

เครื่องปรุง

เนื้อไก่สับหยาบ 3 ถ้วย
เกลือ 1 ช้อนชา พริกป่น 1/2 ช้อนชา
ข้าวคั่วป่นหรือขนมปังป่น 2 ช้อนโต๊ะ
หอมแดงซอย 5 หัว
ต้นหอมหั่นหยาบ 3 ต้น
น้ำมะนาว 1/4 ถ้วย
ใบสะระแหน่เด็ดเป็นใบ 1/4 ถ้วย
ผักชีหั่นหยาบ 2 ช้อนโต๊ะ

วิธีทำ

1. คลุกเนื้อไก่กับเกลือ แล้วใส่ในภาชนะที่เข้าเตาอบได้ ปิดฝา เข้าอบ ในเตาอบ อุณหภูมิ 400°ฟ. นานราว 10 นาที เมื่อเอาออกจากเตาอบ แล้วทิ้งไว้สักครู่ให้เย็นลง แล้วยีเนื้อไก่ให้กระจายออกจากกัน

2. ใส่พริกป่น ข้าวคั่วป่นหรือขนมปังป่น หัวหอม ต้นหอม และน้ำมะนาว ลงไป คลุกให้เข้ากัน ใส่ใบสะระแหน่ ใส่ผักชี คลุกอีกครั้ง ตักใส่จาน เสิร์ฟกับผักกาดหอม ผักกาดขาว แตงกวา ถั่วฝักยาว และต้นหอม

LAP MU
Savory Chopped Pork Salad

ลาบหมู

INGREDIENTS :

2 cups ground lean pork
100 grams pork liver
5-6 tbsp. lime juice
2 tbsp. ground pan-roasted rice or dry breadcrumbs
1/2 tsp. ground chilli
2 tbsp. thinly sliced shallot
2 spring onions, sliced
1 coriander plants, chopped
2 tbsp. fish sauce
1/2 cup mint leaves

PREPARATION :

1. Mix the pork with 4 tbsp. lime juice and work with squeezing movements of the hand; then, squeeze the pork to drive out excess liquid. (Stor liquid for boil) Now, immerse the pork, then put liquid in pan and heated until boiled, stir fried the pork in the boiled liqued until done.

2. Boil the liver until done and then cut into small, thin slices.

3. Mix the pork, liver, pan-roasted rice (or breadcrumbs), ground chilli, shallot, spring onion and coriander plants; season to taste with the fish sauce and the remaining lime juice. Sprinkle with mint leaves and serve with yard-long beans, cabbage, shallot and spring onions.

4 Serving

เครื่องปรุง

หมูเนื้อสันบด 2 ถ้วย
ตับหมู 100 กรัม
น้ำมะนาว 5-6 ช้อนโต๊ะ
ข้าวคั่วป่นหรือขนมปังป่น 2 ช้อนโต๊ะ
พริกป่น 1/2 ช้อนชา
หอมแดงซอย 2 ช้อนโต๊ะ
ต้นหอมซอยหยาบ 2 ต้น
ผักชีซอยหยาบ 1 ต้น
น้ำปลา 2 ช้อนโต๊ะ
ใบสะระแหน่ 1/2 ถ้วย

วิธีทำ

1. ขยำเนื้อหมูกับน้ำมะนาว 4 ช้อนโต๊ะ แล้วบีบเอาเนื้อหมูขึ้นก่อน ใส่น้ำ ที่คั้นออกมาลงในกะทะ ตั้งไฟพอเดือด ใส่หมู ผัดพอสุก

2. ต้มตับหมูให้สุกทั้งชิ้น แล้วหั่นเป็นชิ้นเล็ก บาง

3. ผสมหมู ตับ กับข้าวคั่วป่น (หรือขนมปังป่น) พริกป่น หัวหอม ต้นหอม ผักชี แล้วปรุงรสด้วยน้ำปลา และน้ำมะนาวที่เหลือ ใช้ใบสะระแหน่โรย ข้างหน้า เสิร์ฟกับกะหล่ำปลี ถั่วฝักยาว และต้นหอม

PHLA MU OP
(Savory Baked Pork Salad)

พล่าหมูอบ

INGREDIENTS :

500 grams loinpork
4 lemon grass stems. Take only the swollen base of the stem, where it is tinged with purple and slice thin.
5 thinly sliced shallots
3 kaffir lime leaves, sliced into thin strips
3 tbsp. chopped coriander greens
1/2 cup mint leaves
3 tbsp. thinly sliced spring onion
10 hot chillies
15 cloves garlic
1/2 tsp. salt
4 tbsp. lime juice
1 tbsp. fish sauce
1/2 tsp. sugar
1 tbsp. seasoning sauce
1 tbsp. whiskey
1 tsp. ground black pepper
1 lettuce
5 fried dried chillies.

PREPARATION :

1. Pound the chillies and garlic together with the salt well in mortar and then add the lime juice, fish sauce and sugar to give the dressing a pleasing flavor.

2. Cut the pork into 1-inch pieces, add seasoning sauce, pepper, whiskey and marinate for 30 minutes, place in an oven-proof dish, and bake at 450°F for 10 minutes.

3. Place the pork in a mixing bowl, add the prepared lemon grass, shallots, kaffir lime leaves, coriander greens, mint leaves and spring onion; pour on the dressing. Toss well, then dip onto a plate and serve with lettuce and fried dried chillies.

| 4 Serving |

เครื่องปรุง

หมูสันใน 500 กรัม
ตะไคร้ซอย 4 ต้น
หอมแดงซอย 5 หัว
ใบมะกรูดหั่นฝอย 3 ใบ
ผักชีหั่นหยาบ 3 ช้อนโต๊ะ
ใบสะระแหน่ 1/2 ถ้วย
ต้นหอมซอยหยาบ 3 ช้อนโต๊ะ
พริกขี้หนู 10 เม็ด
กระเทียม 15 กลีบ เกลือ 1/2 ช้อนชา
น้ำมะนาว 4 ช้อนโต๊ะ น้ำปลา 1 ช้อนโต๊ะ
น้ำตาล 1 ช้อนชา ซอสปรุงรส 1 ช้อนโต๊ะ
วิสกี้ 1 ช้อนโต๊ะ พริกไทยดำป่น 1 ช้อนชา
ผักกาดหอม 1 ต้น
พริกแห้งทอด 5 เม็ด

วิธีทำ

1. ทำน้ำปรุงรส โดยโขลกพริกกับกระเทียมและเกลือ แล้วเติมน้ำมะนาว น้ำปลา น้ำตาล คนจนน้ำตาลละลาย

2. หั่นหมูเป็นชิ้น ๆ ยาวชิ้นละ 1 นิ้ว เติมซอสปรุงรส วิสกี้ พริกไทย เคล้าให้เข้ากัน หมักไว้สักครู่ เอาหมูเข้าเตาอบ อบไฟ 450°ฟ นาน 10 นาที

3. คลุกหมูกับตะไคร้ หัวหอม ใบมะกรูด ผักชี ใบสะระแหน่ ต้นหอม และน้ำปรุงรส เคล้าให้ทั่วแล้วตักใส่จาน เสิร์ฟกับผักสดเช่น ต้นหอม ผักชี ผักกาดหอม แต่งด้วยพริกแห้งทอดกรอบ

YAM PLA MEUK
(Spicy Squid Salad)

ยำปลาหมึก

INGREDIENTS FOR DRESSING :

2 tbsp. sliced garlic
2-3 hot chillies
1/4 cup lime juice
3-4 tbsp. fish sauce

PREPARATION :

Pound the chillies and garlic well in a mortar and then mix with the lime juice and fish sauce.

INGREDIENTS :

300 grams fresh squid
1/4 cup thinly sliced shallots
1/4 cup thinly sliced young ginger
1/4 cup thinly sliced lemon grass stems
1 tbsp. chopped spring onion
1/4 cup mint leaves

PREPARATION :

1. Wash the squid, remove the bone, eyes, and the skin. Cut across the squid into about 1 cm. thick rings or score (i.e., make shallow cuts with knife the outer surface of the squid in a criss-cross pattern) and cut into 1 1/2 -inch pieces.

2. Scald the squid in boiling water. Do not leave the squid in the water long, for it will become tough.

3. Gently toss the squid together with the shallots, ginger, spring onion, lemon grass and the dressing and if necessary, season with additional fish sauce or lime juice.

4. Spoon the squid onto a platter, and sprinkle with mint leaves and serve with lettuce, cabbage, etc.

3 Serving

เครื่องปรุงน้ำปรุงรส

กระเทียมซอย 2 ช้อนโต๊ะ พริกขี้หนู 2-3 เม็ด
น้ำมะนาว 1/4 ถ้วย น้ำปลา 3-4 ช้อนโต๊ะ

วิธีทำ

โขลกกระเทียมกับพริกขี้หนูพอแหลก แล้วผสมกับน้ำมะนาวและน้ำปลา เป็นน้ำปรุงรส

เครื่องปรุงอื่น ๆ

ปลาหมึกสด 300 กรัม
หอมแดงซอย 1/4 ถ้วย ขิงอ่อนซอย 1/4 ถ้วย
ตะไคร้ซอย 1/4 ถ้วย
ต้นหอมซอย 1 ช้อนโต๊ะ
ใบสะระแหน่ 1/4 ถ้วย

วิธีทำ

1. ล้างปลาหมึก เอากระดูก ตา และลอกหนังออก บั้งแล้วหั่นเป็นชิ้นกว้าง ราว 1/2 นิ้ว

2. ลวกปลาหมึกในน้ำเดือด พอสุกตักขึ้น อย่าแช่นานจะเหนียว

3. คลุกปลาหมึก กับหัวหอม ตะไคร้ ขิง ต้นหอม และน้ำปรุงรสแต่เพียงเบามือ ปรุงรสด้วยน้ำปลา น้ำมะนาวตามชอบ ตักใส่จานโรยใบสะระแหน่ รับประทาน ทันทีกับผักกาดหอม กะหล่ำปลี และอื่น ๆ

PHLA KUNG
(Savory Prawn Salad)
พล่ากุ้ง

INGREDIENTS :

500 grams prawns	
5 hot chillies	
2 stems lemon grass	
3 shallots	
3 mint plants	
2 shredded kaffir lime leaves	
1 tbsp. lime juice	
1 tbsp. fish sauce	
cabbage	
lettuce	

PREPARATION :

1. Wash, shell, and devein the prawns. Immerse for a short time in boiling water; the prawns should be not quite done.
2. Slice the chillies, lemon grass, and shallots thin.
3. Pick the leaves from the mint plants. Wash them and then drain.
4. Toss the prawns with the lime juice and fish sauce. Add the lemon grass, chilli, shallot, and kaffir lime leaves and toss to mix. The flavor should be spicy.
5. Transfer to a serving dish and garnish with mint leaves. And serve with cabbage and lettuce.

2-3 *Serving*

เครื่องปรุง

กุ้ง 500 กรัม	
พริกขี้หนู 5 เม็ด	
ตะไคร้ 2 ต้น	
หอมแดง 3 หัว	
ใบสะระแหน่ 3 ต้น	
ใบมะกรูดหั่นฝอย 2 ใบ	
น้ำมะนาว 1 ช้อนโต๊ะ	
น้ำปลา 1 ช้อนโต๊ะ	
กะหล่ำปลี	
ผักกาดหอม	

วิธีทำ

1. ล้างกุ้ง แกะเปลือก ชักเส้นดำ แล้วลวกพอสุก
2. ซอยพริก ตะไคร้ และหอมแดง
3. เด็ดใบสะระแหน่ ล้างน้ำ ทิ้งไว้ให้สะเด็ดน้ำ
4. คลุกกุ้งกับน้ำมะนาวและน้ำปลา ใส่ตะไคร้ พริก หอมแดง และใบมะกรูดหั่นฝอย เคล้าให้เข้ากัน
5. ตักใส่จาน แต่งด้วยสะระแหน่ เสิร์ฟกับกะหล่ำปลี ผักกาดหอม

NEUA NAM TOK
(Savory Beef Salad)
เนื้อน้ำตก

INGREDIENTS :

500 grams round beef
1 tbsp. thinly sliced lemon grass
1 1/2 tbsp. ground pan roasted rice
1/4 cup thinly sliced shallot
1/4 cup mint leaves
1/4 cup chopped coriander greens
1 tbsp. chopped spring onion
1/2 tsp. ground dried chilli
3 tbsp. fish sauce
4 1/2 tbsp. lime juice
1/4 tsp. sugar
lettuce, cabbage, spring onion

PREPARATION :

1. Grill beef to medium rare, then cut into thin strips about 1 inch wide.

2. In a mixing bowl, mix all remaining ingredients, blend well, add beef and toss well.

3. Serve the beef with lettuce, cabbage, spring onion etc.

4 Serving

เครื่องปรุง

เนื้อวัวตะโพก 500 กรัม
ตะไคร้ซอยละเอียด 1 ช้อนโต๊ะ
ข้าวคั่วป่น 1 1/2 ช้อนโต๊ะ
หอมแดงซอย 1/4 ถ้วย
ใบสะระแหน่ 1/4 ถ้วย
ผักชีซอยหยาบ 1/4 ถ้วย
ต้นหอมซอยหยาบ 1 ช้อนโต๊ะ
พริกป่น 1/2 ช้อนชา น้ำปลา 3 ช้อนโต๊ะ
น้ำมะนาว 4 1/2 ช้อนโต๊ะ
น้ำตาลทราย 1/4 ช้อนชา
ผักกาดหอม กะหล่ำปลี หอมใบ

วิธีทำ

1. ย่างเนื้อให้สุกปานกลาง หั่นเป็นชิ้นเล็ก ๆ กว้าง 1 นิ้ว

2. ผสมเครื่องปรุงอื่น ๆ ในชามผสมอาหาร ใส่เนื้อลงไปคลุกให้เข้ากัน

3. เสิร์ฟกับผักกาดหอม กะหล่ำปลี และต้นหอม

KUNG PHAO
(Charcoal-Broiled Large Prawns with Savory Sauce)
กุ้งเผา

INGREDIENTS :

3 large prawns
1/3 cup water
1 tbsp. sugar
1/2 tsp. salt
1 1/2 tbsp. chopped garlic
1/2 tbsp. chopped chillies
1 tsp. chopped fresh coriander
2 tbsp. lime juice
foil or banana leaf

PREPARATION :

1. Clean the prawns, wrap each in foil or banana leaf, and tie well. Grill over a charcoal fire about 12 minutes. Serve with the sauce.

2. Heat the sugar and water in a sauce pan over low heat, stirring until the sugar is dissolved. Turn off the heat, add the salt and stir well. Remove from heat and allow to cool; then, add the rest of the ingredients and mix thoroughly.

4 Serving

เครื่องปรุง

กุ้ง 3 ตัว
น้ำ 1/3 ถ้วย
น้ำตาล 1 ช้อนโต๊ะ เกลือ 1/2 ช้อนชา
กระเทียมสับละเอียด 1 1/2 ช้อนโต๊ะ
พริกสับละเอียด 1/2 ช้อนโต๊ะ
ผักชีหั่นละเอียด 1 ช้อนชา
น้ำมะนาว 2 ช้อนโต๊ะ
แผ่นอลูมิเนียมฟอยล์หรือใบตอง

วิธีทำ

1. ล้างกุ้ง ห่อด้วยใบตองเป็นตัว ๆ มัดให้ดี ย่างบนเตาถ่าน ประมาณ 12 นาที เสิร์ฟกับน้ำจิ้ม

2. เอาน้ำกับน้ำตาลใส่หม้อตั้งไฟอ่อนคนจนน้ำตาลละลาย ปิดไฟเติมเกลือ แล้วคนให้ละลายเข้ากัน ยกลง ทิ้งไว้ให้เย็น แล้วใส่เครื่องปรุงอื่นผสมให้ เข้ากันดี เป็นน้ำจิ้ม

KAI KOLAE
(Southern-Thai-Style Braised Chicken)
ไก่กอและ

SPICE MIXTURE INGREDIENTS :

5 dried chillies, seeds removed and soaked in water
2 tbsp. thinly sliced shallot
1 tbsp. chopped garlic
1 tsp. salt
1 tsp. chopped fresh turmeric or curry powder
1/4 tsp. ground roasted coriander seed
1/4 tsp. ground cinnamon
1/4 tsp. ground roasted cumin seed
1 tsp. shrimp paste
or 3 tbsp. red curry paste mix with
1 tsp. turmeric or curry powder

OTHER INGREDIENTS :

1 young chicken 1 1/2 kg.
5 cups coconut milk
4 tbsp. butter
2 tbsp. cooking oil
3 tbsp. fish sauce
3 tbsp. lime juice
2 tbsp. palm sugar

PREPARATION :

1. Pound the chillies and salt in a mortar. Add the garlic and shallot and pound well; then add the turmeric (or curry powder) and pound fine. Add the coriander, cumin, and cinnamon and pound to mix well. Finally, add the shrimp paste and mix in thoroughly.

2. Clean the chicken, cut into 10-12 pieces, and fry in the butter and cooking oil. When the chicken is golden brown transfer it to a pot, add the coconut milk, and place on a medium heat. When the coconut milk comes to a boil, reduce the heat and simmer for 30 minutes.

3. Place the butter and oil remaining from the frying of the chicken in a wok on a medium heat, and fry the spice mixture. When fragrant, add to the pot and season with fish sauce, lime juice, and palm sugar.

4. When the chicken is tender, dip into a serving bowl, garnish with red chillies, and serve with hot rice.

4-5 Serving

เครื่องปรุงน้ำพริก

พริกแห้ง เอาเมล็ดออก แล้วแช่น้ำ 5 เม็ด
หอมแดงซอยละเอียด 2 ช้อนโต๊ะ
กระเทียมสับ 1 ช้อนโต๊ะ เกลือ 1 ช้อนชา
ขมิ้นสดหั่นละเอียด หรือผงกะหรี่ 1 ช้อนชา
เมล็ดผักชีคั่วแล้วบด 1/4 ช้อนชา
อบเชยคั่วแล้วบด 1/4 ช้อนชา
ลูกจันทน์คั่วแล้วบด 1/4 ช้อนชา กะปิ 1 ช้อนชา
หรือ ใช้เครื่องแกงเผ็ด 3 ช้อนโต๊ะ ผสมผงขมิ้นหรือผงกะหรี่ 1 ช้อนชา

เครื่องปรุงอื่น ๆ

ไก่สาวหนักราว 1 1/2 กิโลกรัม 1 ตัว
กะทิ 5 ถ้วย เนย 4 ช้อนโต๊ะ
น้ำมันพืช 2 ช้อนโต๊ะ น้ำปลา 3 ช้อนโต๊ะ
น้ำมะนาว 3 ช้อนโต๊ะ น้ำตาลปีบ 2 ช้อนโต๊ะ

วิธีทำ

1. โขลกน้ำพริก เริ่มด้วยพริกกับเกลือ แล้วใส่หอม กระเทียม ขมิ้น (หรือผงกะหรี่) เมล็ดผักชี อบเชย ลูกจันทน์ เมื่อละเอียดดีแล้วจึงใส่กะปิ โขลกให้เข้ากัน

2. ล้างไก่ สับไก่เป็นชิ้นใหญ่ ๆ ประมาณ 10-12 ชิ้น ทอดกับเนยและน้ำมัน เมื่อเหลืองดีแล้วตักขึ้นใส่หม้อ ใส่กะทิลงไปในหม้อไก่ ยกตั้งไฟปานกลาง เมื่อกะทิเดือด หรี่ไฟเคี่ยวต่อไปประมาณ 30 นาที

3. ตั้งกระทะที่มีเนยและน้ำมันเหลือจากการทอดไก่บนเตา ใช้ไฟปานกลาง ผัดน้ำพริกจนหอม ตักน้ำพริกลงผสมกับกะทิและไก่ ปรุงรสด้วยน้ำปลา น้ำมะนาว และน้ำตาลปีบ

4. เมื่อเนื้อไก่สุกนุ่มดีแล้ว ตักใส่ชาม แต่งด้วยพริกแดง รับประทานกับข้าวร้อน ๆ

PET THOT SOT SAI
(Baked Stuffed Duck)
เป็ดถอดสอดไส้

INGREDIENTS :

1 deboned duck with innards
2 1/2 cups chopped pork   1 egg
2 tbsp. pounded mixture of garlic, coriander root, and pepper
1/4 cup diced onion
1/4 cup diced carrot
1/4 cup peas
3 tbsp. light soy sauce
2 tbsp. seasoning sauce
2 tbsp. butter
1 tbsp. sugar

PREPARATION :

1. Wash the duck, remove the innards and pluck well. Dice the liver, gizzard, heart, and whatever other organs you like. Using a sharp knife with a small, pointed blade debone the duck. Try to keep as much meat as possible and avoid puncturing the meat with the knife. Start near the vent and work up one side toward the neck. Remove the neck and continue around the neck across the back of the duck. Then, follow the same procedure on the other side. Lift the skeleton free of the flesh and then remove the bones from the legs. When done, turn the duck right side out.

2. Mix the pork, pounded garlic mixture, diced innards, peas, carrot, and onion together well, add the egg and mix in, and season with sugar, light soy sauce, and seasoning sauce. Fill the cavities of the duck with the mixture, sew the duck closed, and tie securely with thread around the outside into a long, cigarshaped configuration.

3. Place the duck in a baking pan and bake at 350°F for 40 minutes. Remove the duck from the oven, spread the butter over the outside, and bake at 400°F for 20 minutes. When the back of the duck has turned dark brown, remove from the oven, allow to cool, and cut into 1/2 - inch slices.

4. Place the slices on a bed of lettuce on a serving platter, surround with slices of tomato, and onion and spoon gravy over the duck.

INGREDIENTS FOR GRAVY :

1/4 cup juice from the pan in which the duck was baked
1 tbsp. wheat flour 1/4 tsp. salt 1/8 tsp. pepper

PREPARATION :

Heat the duck juice in a wok over low heat. Add the flour, salt, and pepper and stir until the gravy is smooth.

8 Serving

เครื่องปรุง

เป็ดพร้อมเครื่องใน 1 ตัว หมูสับ 2 1/2 ถ้วย ไข่ไก่ 1 ฟอง
รากผักชี กระเทียม พริกไทยโขลกละเอียด 2 ช้อนโต๊ะ
เมล็ดถั่วลันเตา 1/4 ถ้วย แครอทหั่นเป็นชิ้นสี่เหลี่ยมเล็ก 1/4 ถ้วย
หอมใหญ่หั่นเป็นชิ้นสี่เหลี่ยมเล็ก 1/4 ถ้วย
ซีอิ๊วขาว 3 ช้อนโต๊ะ ซอสปรุงรส 2 ช้อนโต๊ะ
เนยสด 2 ช้อนโต๊ะ น้ำตาลทราย 1 ช้อนโต๊ะ

วิธีทำ

1. ล้างเป็ด ถอนขนให้เกลี้ยง เอาเครื่องในออก

2. ล้างเครื่องใน หั่นตับ กึ๋น หัวใจเป็นชิ้นเล็ก

3. ถอดกระดูกเป็ดโดยใช้มีดเล็กปลายแหลมและคม ให้เนื้อเป็ดติดกระดูกไปน้อยที่สุดและระวังไม่ให้เนื้อเป็ดขาด โดยเริ่มกรีดจากช่องท้องขึ้นไปหาส่วนคอ ตัดคอทิ้ง แล้วเลาะไปรอบคอลงไปหาส่วนหลังทำเช่นเดียวกันอีกข้างหนึ่ง ดึงโครงกระดูกออกจากส่วนลำตัวซึ่งจะทำให้ด้านในกลับออกมาด้านนอก เลาะกระดูกขา แล้วกลับด้านในเข้าตามเดิม

4. ผสมหมูสับกับกระเทียม รากผักชี และพริกไทยโขลก รวมทั้งเครื่องในเป็ด ถั่ว แครอท และหัวหอมเข้าด้วยกัน ตอกไข่ใส่ ปรุงรสด้วยน้ำตาล ซีอิ๊วและซอสปรุงรส คลุกให้เข้ากันดี แล้วนำไปยัดไส้เป็ดแล้วเย็บปิดช่องท้องให้แน่น จะได้เป็ดยัดไส้เป็นท่อนกลมยาว

5. วางเป็ดในถาดอบ นำเข้าเตาอบอุณหภูมิ 350°ฟ เป็นเวลา 40 นาที แล้วเอาเป็ดออกจากเตาอบ เอาเนยทาแล้วอบต่อ 20 นาที อุณหภูมิ 400°ฟ เมื่อส่วนหลังของเป็ดเกรียมดีแล้วเอาออก พักไว้ให้เย็น หั่นเป็นแว่น ๆ หนาแว่นละ 1/2 นิ้ว

6. เรียงชิ้นเป็ดสอดไส้ลงบนใบผักกาดขาวที่ปูรองกับจานเสิร์ฟ แต่งด้วยมะเขือเทศ และหอมหัวใหญ่ หั่นเป็นแว่น ราดด้วยน้ำเกรวี่

วิธีทำน้ำเกรวี่

ใส่น้ำจากตัวเป็ดลงในกระทะ 1/4 ถ้วย ตั้งไฟอ่อน สักครู่ใส่แป้งสาลี 1 ช้อนโต๊ะ เกลือ 1/4 ช้อนชา และพริกไทย 1/8 ช้อนชา คนให้แป้งและเกลือละลายเป็นเนื้อเดียวกัน

KAI OP NAM DAENG
(Braised Chicken)
ไก่อบน้ำแดง

INGREDIENTS :

500 grams chicken breasts, thighs, or drumsticks
1 tsp. salt
1/4 tsp. pepper
1/2 cup cooking oil
2 tbsp. chopped onion
1 tbsp. catsup
1 tbsp. seasoning sauce
1 tbsp. light soy sauce
1 tbsp. Worcestershire sauce
1 tbsp. medium hot chilli sauce
2 tbsp. sugar
3 bay leaves
1 cup water
1 cup boiled green beans or carrots

PREPARATION :

1. Wash the chicken and allow to dry or dry with absorbent paper.

2. Mix the salt and pepper and spread over all the chicken parts with the hand. Heat the oil in a wok, fry the chicken until golden, and then remove from the wok and drain.

3. Return the wok with the remaining oil to the heat and fry the onion. When fragrant, add the catsup, seasoning sauce, soy sauce, Worcestershire sauce, chilli sauce and sugar, stir, then transfer to a pot.

4. Place the chicken and the water in the pot, add bay leaves. Cover and simmer over low heat until the chicken is tender. Serve with boiled green beans or carrots.

3 Serving

เครื่องปรุง

เนื้อไก่ส่วนอก โคนขา หรือน่อง 500 กรัม
เกลือ 1 ช้อนชา พริกไทยป่น 1/4 ช้อนชา
น้ำมันพืช 1/2 ถ้วย
หอมใหญ่สับละเอียด 2 ช้อนโต๊ะ
ซอสมะเขือเทศ 1 ช้อนโต๊ะ
ซอสปรุงรส 1 ช้อนโต๊ะ ซีอิ๊วขาว 1 ช้อนโต๊ะ
ซอสไก่งวง 1 ช้อนโต๊ะ
ซอสพริกเผ็ดกลาง 1 ช้อนโต๊ะ
น้ำตาล 2 ช้อนโต๊ะ
ใบกระวาน 3 ใบ น้ำ 1 ถ้วย
ถั่วแขกหรือแครอทต้ม 1 ถ้วย

วิธีทำ

1. ล้างไก่ ผึ่งไว้หรือซับน้ำให้แห้ง

2. ผสมเกลือกับพริกไทยแล้วคลุกไก่ให้ทั่วทั้งชิ้นก่อนนำไปทอดจนเหลืองดี ตักขึ้นพักไว้ให้สะเด็ดน้ำมัน

3. เจียวหอมด้วยน้ำมันที่เหลือจากทอดไก่ เมื่อหอมดีแล้วใส่ซอสมะเขือเทศ ซอสปรุงรส ซีอิ๊ว ซอสไก่งวง ซอสพริก น้ำตาล ใบกระวาน คนให้เข้ากัน ตักลงใส่หม้อ

4. ใส่ไก่ลงในหม้อ เติมน้ำใส่ใบกระวานปิดฝา เคี่ยวโดยใช้ไฟอ่อนจนไก่ สุกนุ่ม เสิร์ฟกับถั่วแขกหรือแครอทต้มสุก

PET OP KROP
(Crispy Baked Duck)
เป็ดอบกรอบ

INGREDIENTS :

1 duck weighing about 1 1/2 kg. - 2 kg.
2 tsp. minced mature ginger
1 tsp. ground cinnamon
1/2 tsp. nutmeg
1 tsp. pepper
2 tbsp. light soy sauce

PREPARATION :

1. Wash the duck, remove the neck, feet, and innards, and pat dry.

2. Mix the ginger, cinnamon, nutmeg, and pepper. Take 1 tsp. of this mixture and spread it over the inside of the duck; then, sew the duck securely closed. Spread the remainder of the spice mixture over the outside of the duck.

3. Wrap the duck in aluminum foil, place it in a deep roasting pan, bake at 450°F. for one hour. After taking the duck from the oven, allow it to cool about fifteen minutes before removing the aluminum foil.

4. Place the duck on a roasting rack and put it on a cookie sheet. With a fork, puncture the skin of the duck at many places over the entire surface in order to prevent the skin's cracking.

5. Bake the duck at 350°F. for about 30 minutes. Remove the duck from the oven and brush the skin with the light soy sauce. Now, bake at 500°F. for about 5 minutes, until the skin is crisp and brown. Do not allow it to burn.

6. Serve the duck either split in half or deboned. Alternatively, the skin may be served without the meat. Serve with spring onions, cucumbers, lettuce, and celery and dark soy sauce.

> 4 Serving

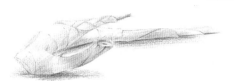

เครื่องปรุง

เป็ดหนักประมาณ 1 1/2 ก.ก. - 2 ก.ก. 1 ตัว
ขิงแก่สับละเอียด 2 ช้อนชา
อบเชยป่น 1 ช้อนชา
ลูกจันทน์ป่น 1/2 ช้อนชา
พริกไทยป่น 1 ช้อนชา ซีอิ๊วขาว 2 ช้อนโต๊ะ

วิธีทำ

1. ล้างเป็ด ถอนขนให้เกลี้ยง ไม่เอาคอ ตีนและเครื่องใน ล้างแล้วซับน้ำให้แห้ง

2. ผสมขิง อบเชย ลูกจันทน์ และพริกไทยเข้าด้วยกัน นำส่วนผสมนี้ 1 ช้อนชาไปทาด้านในช่องท้องของตัวเป็ดให้ทั่วก่อนจะเย็บปิดช่องท้องให้แน่นหนา ส่วนผสมขิง อบเชย ลูกจันทน์และพริกไทยที่เหลือใช้ทาให้ทั่วภายนอกตัวเป็ด

3. ห่อเป็ดด้วยแผ่นอะลูมิเนียมฟอยล์ วางลงในถาดอบลึก ๆ นำเข้าเตาอบ อุณหภูมิ 450°ฟ. อบนาน 1 ชั่วโมง เมื่อเอาเป็ดออกจากเตาอบแล้วทิ้งไว้ประมาณ 15 นาทีให้เย็นแล้วจึงแกะแผ่นฟอยล์ออก

4. วางเป็ดลงบนตะแกรงอบรองด้วยกระดาษรองถาดคุ้กกี้ ใช้ส้อมจิ้มหนังเป็ดให้เป็นรูทั่วตัวเพื่อป้องกันไม่ให้หนังเป็ดแตกก่อนจะเอาเป็ดเข้าอบ อุณหภูมิ 350°ฟ. อีก 30 นาที แล้วเอาเป็ดออกจากเตาอบ ใช้ซีอิ๊วทาให้ทั่วตัวเป็ด

5. อบเป็ดอีกครั้งหนึ่ง อุณหภูมิ 500°ฟ. นาน 5 นาที หนังเป็ดจะเกรียมกรอบ ระวังอย่าให้ไหม้

6. จะผ่าเป็ดเป็น 2 ซีกหรือถอดกระดูกก่อนเสิร์ฟก็ได้ หรืออาจแยกหนังออกก็ได้ รับประทานกับต้นหอม แตงกวา ผักกาดหอม ขึ้นฉ่ายและซีอิ๊วหวาน

KAI YANG
(Thai-Style Barbecued Chicken)
ไก่ย่าง

INGREDIENTS :

1 kg. chicken pieces
2 tbsp. chopped fresh ginger
2 tbsp. chopped lemon grass
2 tbsp. chopped coriander root
2 cups light soy sauce
1 tsp. sugar
2 tbsp. pepper
1 1/2 tbsp. curry powder

PREPARATION :

1. Mix all the ingredients, except the chicken, in a blender, and marinate the chicken in the mixture for at least 6 hours in a refrigerator.
2. Broil the chicken slowly over a low fire and serve with sweet chilli sauce.

INGREDIENTS FOR SWEET CHILLI SAUCE :

1 tbsp. ground red chilli
1/2 cup vinegar
1/2 tsp. salt
1 tbsp. sugar
1 tsp. chopped garlic

PREPARATION :

Mix all the ingredients in a small pot, put over a medium heat and bring to a boil, stirring. Heat until thickened to a syrupy consistency then remove from heat.

4 Serving

เครื่องปรุง

ไก่ส่วนต่าง ๆ เป็นชิ้น ๆ 1 กิโลกรัม
ขิงสับละเอียด 2 ช้อนโต๊ะ
ตะไคร้สับละเอียด 2 ช้อนโต๊ะ
รากผักชีสับละเอียด 2 ช้อนโต๊ะ
ซีอิ๊วขาว 2 ถ้วย
น้ำตาลทราย 1 ช้อนชา
พริกไทย 2 ช้อนโต๊ะ
ผงกะหรี่ 1 1/2 ช้อนโต๊ะ

วิธีทำ
1. ผสมเครื่องเทศต่าง ๆ เข้าด้วยกันโดยใช้เครื่องปั่น
2. หมักไก่ในส่วนผสมดังกล่าว ทิ้งไว้ในตู้เย็นนานประมาณ 6 ชั่วโมง
3. ย่างไก่ให้สุก เกรียมตามชอบ ใช้ไฟอ่อน
4. รับประทานกับน้ำจิ้มไก่ย่าง

วิธีทำน้ำจิ้ม
ผสมพริกแดงโขลก 1 ช้อนโต๊ะ น้ำส้มสายชู 1/2 ถ้วย เกลือ 1/2 ช้อนชา น้ำตาลทราย 1 ช้อนโต๊ะ กระเทียมโขลกหรือสับ 1 ช้อนชา ตั้งไฟ เคี่ยว จนเดือด หมั่นคน เคี่ยวต่อจนน้ำจิ้มข้นเป็นน้ำเชื่อมจึงยกลง

KUNG YANG SOT MAKHAM PIAK
(Broiled Lobsters in Tamarind Sauce)
กุ้งย่างซอสมะขามเปียก

INGREDIENTS :

500 grams lobsters or large prawns
1/2 tbsp. palm sugar
1 1/2 tbsp. fish sauce
1/4 tsp. salt
1 tbsp. chopped coriander root
1/3 cup thinly sliced shallot
1 coriander green
2 1/2 tbsp. tamarind juice
1 1/2 tbsp. vegetable oil
1 tbsp. finely chopped garlic
1 tbsp. water

PREPARATION :

1. Put the oil in a wok over medium heat. Sauté the garlic, shallot and coriander root until fragrant. Set aside in the wok.

2. Mix the palm sugar, tamarind juice, salt, fish sauce and water in the wok. When the mixture comes to a boil, add the fried garlic, shallot and coriander. Mix well. Bring to a boil again, then remove from heat.

3. Broil the lobsters and shell them. Arrange on a serving platter, then pour the sauce over them. Just before serving, sprinkle with corainder leaves.

เครื่องปรุง

กุ้งมังกรหรือกุ้งกร้ามกรามขนาดใหญ่เผาให้สุกแล้วแกะเปลือก เอาเส้นดำออก 500 กรัม
น้ำตาลปีบ 1/2 ช้อนโต๊ะ
น้ำปลา 1 1/2 ช้อนโต๊ะ
เกลือ 1/4 ช้อนชา
รากผักชีสับละเอียด 1 ช้อนโต๊ะ
หอมแดงซอย 1/3 ถ้วย
ผักชีเด็ดเอาแต่ใบเป็นช่อ ๆ 1 ต้น
น้ำส้มมะขามเปียก 2 1/2 ช้อนโต๊ะ
น้ำมันพืช 1 1/2 ช้อนโต๊ะ
กระเทียมสับละเอียด 1 ช้อนโต๊ะ
น้ำ 1 ช้อนโต๊ะ

วิธีทำ

1. เจียวกระเทียม หอมแดง และรากผักชีในน้ำมัน ใช้ไฟปานกลางจนหอม ดีแล้วตักขึ้นพักไว้ข้างกระทะ

2. ผสมน้ำตาล น้ำส้มมะขาม เกลือ น้ำปลาและน้ำในกระทะตั้งไฟพอเดือด ใส่กระเทียม หอมและรากผักชีเขียว พอเดือดยกลง ใช้เป็นซอสมะขามเปียก

3. กุ้งเผาแกะเปลือกผ่ากลางตัวแบะออก จัดกุ้งลงจาน ราดด้วยน้ำซอสให้ ทั่ว แต่งหน้าด้วยผักชี

SI-KHRONG MU YANG
(Barbecued Spareribs)
ซี่โครงหมูย่าง

INGREDIENTS :

1 kg. spareribs	
3 tbsp. light soy sauce	
3 tbsp. whiskey	
1 tsp. salt	
1/4 tsp. ground nutmeg	
1/4 tsp. ground cinnamon	
1 1/2 tbsp. minced ginger	
1 tsp. pepper	

PREPARATION :

1. Cut the spareribs into pieces about 5 inches long and about 3 inches-or three ribs-wide.

2. Sprinkle the soy sauce and whiskey onto the spareribs so as to wet all surfaces. Mix the salt, nutmeg, cinnamon, ginger, and pepper together and then smear the mixture onto the ribs, covering them completely. Set aside to marinate for an hour.

3. Broil the spareribs over a low charcoal until the meat is done and golden brown.

4. Cut the ribs into 2 inches pieces and serve with pineapple, spring onions and lettuce.

4 Serving

เครื่องปรุง

ซี่โครงหมู 1 กิโลกรัม	
ซีอิ๊วขาว 3 ช้อนโต๊ะ	
วิสกี้ 3 ช้อนโต๊ะ เกลือ 1 ช้อนชา	
ลูกจันทน์ป่น 1/4 ช้อนชา	
อบเชยป่น 1/4 ช้อนชา	
ขิงสับละเอียด 1 1/2 ช้อนโต๊ะ	
พริกไทย 1 ช้อนชา	

วิธีทำ

1. สับซี่โครงหมูเป็นท่อน ๆ ยาวประมาณ 4-5 นิ้ว กว้าง 3 นิ้วหรือ 3 ซี่

2. ราดซีอิ๊วกับวิสกี้ให้ทั่วซี่โครงหมูแต่ละชิ้น

3. ผสมเกลือ ลูกจันทน์ป่น อบเชยป่น ขิง และพริกไทยเข้าด้วยกัน ทาซี่โครงหมูให้ทั่ว ตั้งหมักไว้ราว 1 ชั่วโมง

4. ย่างซี่โครงหมู โดยใช้เตาถ่าน ไฟอ่อนจนสุกเกรียม

5. สับซี่โครงหมูเป็นชิ้นสั้น ๆ เสิร์ฟกับ สับปะรด ต้นหอม และผักกาดหอม

KHA MU TOM PHALO
(Boiled Fresh Ham with the Five Spices)
ขาหมูต้มพะโล้

INGREDIENTS :

800 grams fresh ham
10 cloves garlic
3 coriander roots 1/2 tsp. five spice powder
20 pepper corns
1 tsp. dark soy sauce
2 tbsp. light soy sauce

PREPARATION :

Place all the ingredients in a pressure cooker and add enough water to nearly cover the ham (about 2 cups). Cover and cook about 20 minutes over medium heat. After removing the pressure cooker from the heat, allow it to cool (at least 10 minutes) before opening. Remove the bone from the ham, place the meat and the liquid in a serving dish, and sprinkle with chopped coriander greens. Serve with the sauce.

INGREDIENTS FOR SAUCE :

2 yellow chillies
1 coriander root
10 cloves garlic
1/4 tsp. salt
2 tbsp. vinegar

PREPARATION :

Place the chillies, coriander root, garlic, and salt in a mortar and break up with the pestle. Add the vinegar, mix, and transfer to a small bowl.

6 Serving

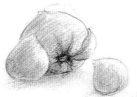

เครื่องปรุง

ขาหมู 800 กรัม
กระเทียม 10 กลีบ
รากผักชี 3 ราก ผงพะโล้ 1/2 ช้อนชา
พริกไทยเม็ด 20 เม็ด
ซีอิ๊วดำ 1ช้อนชา ซีอิ๊วขาว 2 ช้อนโต๊ะ

วิธีทำ

1. ใส่เครื่องปรุงทั้งหมดลงในหม้ออัดความดัน เติมน้ำลงไปจนเกือบท่วม ขาหมู (ประมาณ 2 ถ้วย)

2. ปิดฝาหม้อ ต้มประมาณ 20 นาที ใช้ไฟแรงปานกลางแล้วยกลง พัก ไว้ให้เย็น (ประมาณ 10 นาทีเป็นอย่างน้อย) ก่อนจะเปิดฝาหม้อ

3. เลาะเอาแต่เนื้อ หั่นชิ้นขนาดคำ ตักใส่จาน โรยด้วยผักชี เสิร์ฟกับน้ำจิ้ม

เครื่องปรุงน้ำจิ้ม

พริกเหลือง 2 เม็ด
รากผักชี 1 ราก
กระเทียม 10 กลีบ เกลือ 1/4 ช้อนชา
น้ำส้มสายชู 2 ช้อนโต๊ะ

วิธีทำ

โขลกพริก รากผักชี กระเทียมและเกลือพอแหลก แล้วจึงผสมกับน้ำส้ม

PLA KAO OP
SOT MA-KHEUA THET
(Baked Rock Cod in Tomato Sauce)
ปลาเก๋าอบซอสมะเขือเทศ

INGREDIENTS :

1 medium-sized whole rock cod	
1 tbsp. butter	
1/2 cup tomato sauce	
1 tbsp. dry white wine	
1 1/2 tbsp. fish sauce	
1 tsp. sugar	
1 tsp. pepper	
1 onion, sliced	
1 large tomato, sliced	
2 bell peppers, sliced	
1 foil or whole banana leaf	

PREPARATION :

Lightly butter an 8 by 10 inches piece of foil (or banana leaf). Put cleaned and scaled fish onto the center of the foil. Mix tomato sauce and wine, with the fish sauce, sugar and pepper. Pour the mixture and place all remaining ingredients over the fish. Wrap the fish, sealing it in the foil, tie if necessary, and bake in an oven heated to 350°F. for 15-20 minutes.

2-3 Serving

เครื่องปรุง

ปลาเก๋า ขอดเกล็ด ล้างสะอาดขนาดกลาง 1 ตัว	
เนย 1 ช้อนโต๊ะ ซอสมะเขือเทศ 1/2 ถ้วย	
ไวน์ขาว 1 ช้อนโต๊ะ น้ำปลา 1 1/2 ช้อนโต๊ะ	
น้ำตาลทราย 1 ช้อนชา พริกไทยป่น 1 ช้อนชา	
หอมใหญ่หั่นเป็นแว่น 1 หัว	
มะเขือเทศผลใหญ่หั่นเป็นแว่น 1 ผล	
พริกยักษ์หั่นเป็นแว่น 2 เม็ด	
อลูมิเนียมฟอยล์ หรือใบตอง 1 แผ่น	

วิธีทำ

ทาอลูมิเนียมฟอยล์ (หรือใบตอง) ด้วยเนยบาง ๆ วางปลาเก๋าลงตรงกลาง แผ่นฟอยล์ ราดด้วยซอสมะเขือเทศที่ผสมกับไวน์ น้ำปลา น้ำตาล และ พริกไทยแล้ว เรียงหอมใหญ่ มะเขือเทศ และพริกลงบนตัวปลา พับฟอยล์ หรือใบตองห่อตัวปลา หากจำเป็นอาจใช้เชือกมัด แล้วอบในเตาอบไฟ 350°ฟ ราว 15-20 นาที

PLA O YANG SI IU
(Broiled Tunny with Soy Sauce)
ปลาโอย่างซีอิ๊ว

INGREDIENTS:

1 firm-fleshed tunny weighing about 400 grams
2 tbsp. light soy sauce
lettuce, prickled carrot and Chinese radish

PREPARATION :

1. Wash and clean the fish, allow to drain; then, broil until golden.

2. Place the fish on a platter and pour the soy sauce over it.

3. Serve with fresh or pickled vegetable.

3 Serving

เครื่องปรุง

ปลาโอหนักประมาณ 400 กรัม 1 ตัว
ซีอิ๊วขาว 2 ช้อนโต๊ะ
ผักกาดหอมแครอทดอง และหัวไชเท้า

วิธีทำ

1. ล้างปลาให้สะอาด พักไว้จนสะเด็ดน้ำก่อนนำมาย่าง

2. เมื่อปลาสุกเหลืองดีแล้ว วางปลาลงในจานราดด้วยซีอิ๊วขาว

3. เสิร์ฟกับผักได้ทั้งผักดิบ และผักดอง

LON HAEM
(Coconut Ham Sauce)
หลนแฮม

INGREDIENTS :

400 grams grated coconut or 2 cups coconut milk
1 cup ham cut into small cubes
1/2 cup fermented rice
1/4 tsp. salt
2-3 tbsp. tamarind juice
1 tbsp. palm sugar
1/4 cup minced shallots
6 chillies cut into short lengths
1 coriander green

PREPARATION :

1. Mix 1 cup warm water with the coconut and squeeze out 2 cups coconut milk.

2. Place the coconut milk in a pot with the ham and fermented rice and heat to boiling. Add salt, tamarind juice, and palm sugar to taste; then, add the shallots and chilli. When the sauce comes to a boil, remove from heat, sprinkle with coriander green.

3. Serve with fresh vegetables, such as cucumbers, cabbage, winged beans, yard-long beans, and lettuce.

3 Serving

เครื่องปรุง

มะพร้าวขูด 400 กรัม (หรือกะทิ 2 ถ้วย)
แฮมหั่นเป็นชิ้นสี่เหลี่ยมเล็ก 1 ถ้วย
ข้าวหมาก 1/2 ถ้วย
เกลือ 1/4 ช้อนชา
น้ำส้มมะขาม 2-3 ช้อนโต๊ะ
น้ำตาลปีบ 1 ช้อนโต๊ะ
หอมแดงซอย 1/4 ถ้วย
พริกหั่นหยาบ 6 เม็ด ผักชี 1 ต้น

วิธีทำ

1. ใช้น้ำอุ่น 1 ถ้วยคั้นมะพร้าวให้ได้กะทิ 2 ถ้วย

2. ใส่กะทิในหม้อ ใส่แฮมและข้าวหมาก ตั้งไฟจนเดือด เติมเกลือ น้ำส้ม-มะขาม และน้ำตาลปีบ แล้วจึงใส่หัวหอมและพริก เมื่อเดือดอีกครั้งยกลง โรยหน้าด้วยผักชี

3. เสิร์ฟกับผักสด เช่น แตงกวา กะหล่ำปลี ถั่วพู ถั่วฝักยาว และผักกาดหอม

NAM PHRIK ONG
(Pork and Tomato Chilli Dip)
น้ำพริกอ่อง

INGREDIENTS :

3 tbsp. chopped pork
1 cup sliced cherry tomatoes
5 dried chillies, soaked
1 tsp. salt
1 tbsp. finely sliced galangal
3 tbsp. chopped onion
1 tsp. shrimp paste
5 cloves garlic
3 cloves garlic, chopped
2 tbsp. cooking oil
1 coriander plant
1/2 cup water
Fresh Vegetables :
cucumber, yard-long bean, carrot, eggplant, cabbage, etc.
Boiled Vegetables :
yard-long bean, eggplant, pumpkin vine tip, swamp cabbage, banana blossom, etc.

PREPARATION :

1. Pound the chillies, salt, and galangal well in a mortar. Add the onion, shrimp paste, and the five garlic cloves and pound to mix thoroughly. Add the pork and continue pounding to mix. Finally, add the tomatoes pound to mix well.

2. Heat the oil in a wok. When it is hot, add the chopped garlic. When the garlic is fragrant, add the pork and tomato chilli paste and continue frying over low heat with stirring, until the ingredients take on a gloss; then, add the water.

3. Continue cooking with regular stirring until much of the water evaporates and the mixture becomes fairly thick. Then, transfer to a bowl, sprinkle with chopped coriander leaves and serve with fresh vegetables or boiled vegetables or both.

4 Serving

เครื่องปรุง

หมูสับ 3 ช้อนโต๊ะ
มะเขือเทศสีดา 1 ถ้วย
พริกแห้งตัดเป็นท่อนสั้น ๆ แล้วแช่น้ำ 5 เม็ด
เกลือ 1 ช้อนชา ข่าฝานเป็นชิ้นบาง 1 ช้อนโต๊ะ
หอมใหญ่สับ 3 ช้อนโต๊ะ
กะปิ 1 ช้อนชา กระเทียม 5 กลีบ
กระเทียมสับ 3 กลีบ น้ำมันพืช 2 ช้อนโต๊ะ
ผักชี 1 ต้น น้ำ 1/2 ถ้วย
ผักสด: แตงกวา ถั่วฝักยาว แครอท มะเขือ กะหล่ำปลี ฯลฯ
ผักต้ม: ถั่วฝักยาว มะเขือยาว ยอดฟักทอง ผักบุ้ง หัวปลี ฯลฯ

วิธีทำ

1. โขลกพริก เกลือ และข่าให้ละเอียด แล้วจึงเติมหัวหอม กะปิ และกระเทียม ลงโขลกให้ละเอียดเข้ากัน ใส่เนื้อหมู และท้ายสุดใส่มะเขือเทศลงโขลกด้วย

2. ใส่น้ำมันในกระทะตั้งไฟ พอร้อน เจียวกระเทียมให้เหลือง หอม หรี่ไฟ แล้วตักน้ำพริกผสมหมูใส่กระทะ ผัดต่อจนน้ำมันขึ้นเป็นเงา แล้วจึงเติมน้ำ

3. ผัดต่อไปจนน้ำระเหย และน้ำพริกข้น ตักขึ้นใส่ถ้วย โรยหน้าด้วยผักชี รับประทานได้ทั้งกับผักสดและผักต้ม

MU SA-TE
(Pork Sateh)
หมูสะเต๊ะ

INGREDIENTS :

500 grams lean pork
2 tsp. ground roasted coriander seed
1/2 tsp. ground roasted cumin seed
1 tsp. finely chopped galangal
1 heaping tbsp. finely chopped lemon grass
1 tsp. turmeric
1/4 tsp. ground pepper
1 tsp. salt
2 tsp. sugar
1/2 cup coconut cream
100 skewers

PREPARATION :

1. Cut the meat into thin slices about 1 inch wide and 2 inches long.

2. Pound the coriander seed, cumin, galangal, lemon grass, turmeric, salt, and pepper in mortar until finely ground. Pour over the meat along with the sugar and the coconut cream. Mix throughly, and set aside to marinate 30 minutes.

3. Skewer the meat strips lengthwise and broil over a medium charcoal fire, brushing occasionally with the remaining marinade. Serve with sauce and relish.

INGREDIENTS FOR SATEH SAUCE

1/4 cup red curry paste (See p. 22)
2 cups coconut milk
1/2 cup ground roasted peanuts
1/4 cup sugar
1/4 cup tamarind juice
1 1/2 tsp. salt

PREPARATION:

1. Mix the peanuts and the red curry paste together well.

2. Skim one cup of coconut cream from the coconut milk. Heat the coconut cream in a wok until the oil surfaces; then, add the peanut-curry paste mixture and stir and turn to mix well. Add the remaining coconut milk and reduce the heat. Continue to stir regularly.

3. Season to taste with sugar and tamarind juice, and if you like, with salt. When the sauce has thickened, spoon into a serving bowl.

4 Serving

เครื่องปรุง

เนื้อหมู 500 กรัม ลูกผักชีบด 2 ช้อนชา
ยี่หร่าบด 1/2 ช้อนชา ข่าสับละเอียด 1 ช้อนชา
ตะไคร้ซอย 1 ช้อนโต๊ะพูน ขมิ้น 1 ช้อนชา
พริกไทยป่น 1/4 ช้อนชา เกลือ 1 ช้อนชา
น้ำตาลทราย 2 ช้อนชา หัวกะทิ 1/2 ถ้วย
ไม้สำหรับเสียบ 100 ไม้

วิธีทำ

1. หั่นเนื้อหมูเป็นชิ้นบาง กว้างราว 1 นิ้ว ยาว 2 นิ้ว

2. โขลกลูกผักชี ยี่หร่า ข่า ตะไคร้ ขมิ้น เกลือและพริกไทยให้ละเอียด ใส่เนื้อ น้ำตาลและหัวกะทิลงคลุก แล้วหมักทิ้งไว้ราว 30 นาที

3. เอาเนื้อเสียบไม้ตามยาว ปิ้งโดยใช้เตาถ่าน ไฟแรงปานกลาง ใช้น้ำหมัก เนื้อทาบ้างเป็นครั้งคราว เสิร์ฟกับน้ำจิ้มและอาจาด

เครื่องปรุงน้ำจิ้ม

น้ำพริกแกงแดง (ดูหน้า 22) 1/4 ถ้วย
กะทิ 2 ถ้วย ถั่วลิสงคั่วบด 1/2 ถ้วย
น้ำตาลทราย 1/4 ถ้วย
น้ำส้มมะขาม 1/4 ถ้วย เกลือ 1 1/2 ช้อนชา

วิธีทำ

1. ผสมถั่วลิสงกับน้ำพริกแกงแดง

2. ตักหัวกะทิแยกขึ้นมา 1 ถ้วย ใส่หัวกะทิลงในกระทะตั้งไฟเคี่ยวจนแตก มัน ใส่ถั่วลิสงผสมน้ำพริกลงผัดจนเข้ากันดี เติมกะทิที่เหลือลงไป หรี่ไฟ หมั่นคน

3. ปรุงรสตามชอบด้วยน้ำตาล น้ำส้มมะขาม และอาจเติมเกลือด้วยก็ได้ เมื่อ น้ำจิ้มข้นแล้วตักใส่ถ้วย

SATEH SAUCE

CUCUMBER RELISH

INGREDIENTS FOR CUCUMBER RELISH

4 cucumbers
2 shallots
1 chilli
1/3 cup vinegar
2 tsp. sugar
1/2 tsp. salt
1 tbsp. coriander green, chopped

PREPARATION:

1. Wash the cucumbers, cut in half lengthwise, and then cut across into thin slices. Cut the shallots and chillies into thin slices. Place the cucumber, shallot, and chilli slices in a bowl.

2. Heat the vinegar, sugar and salt, stirring constantly until sugar has dissolved. When the mixture comes to a boil, remove from the heat. After the mixture has cooled, add it to bowl and garnish with chopped coriander greens.

เครื่องปรุงอาจาด

แตงกวา 4 ผล หอมแดง 2 หัว
พริก 1 เม็ด น้ำส้มสายชู 1 1/3 ถ้วย
น้ำตาลทราย 2 ช้อนชา เกลือ 1/4 ช้อนชา
ผักชีหั่นหยาบ 1 ช้อนโต๊ะ

วิธีทำ

1. แตงกวา ล้าง ผ่าครึ่งตามยาวแล้วหั่นขวางเป็นชิ้นบาง ซอยหัวหอมและพริก ใส่แตงกวา หัวหอมและพริกไว้ในถ้วย

2. เอาน้ำส้ม น้ำตาล เกลือ ใส่หม้อเล็กตั้งไฟ หมั่นคนจนน้ำตาลกับเกลือละลาย พอเดือดยกลง ทิ้งไว้ให้เย็นก่อนราดลงในถ้วยแตงกวา โรยผักชี

KHANOM JIN NAM YA
(Vemicelli and Fish Sauce)
ขนมจีนน้ำยา

INGREDIENTS :

7 shallots, cut up coarsely
2 garlic bulbs 2 tsp. sliced galangal
2 tbsp. sliced lemon grass
1 cup minced krachai
3 dried chillies, seeds removed
1 tsp. salt 1 tsp. shrimp paste
1 one-inch thick piece of salted fish, roasted
1 cup water

Place all above in a pot and simmer over low heat until soft. Remove from heat, cool, place in mortar, and pound to a fine paste.

OTHER INGREDIENTS :

400 grams grated coconut or 5 1/2 cups coconut milk
1 meaty fish (200 grams) 2-3 tbsp. fish sauce
2 hard boiled eggs, each peeled and cut into 5 sections
1 kg vermicelli
1/2 cup cabbage, sliced
1/2 cup yard long bean, sliced
1/2 cup cucumber, sliced
1/2 cup boiled bean sprouts
1 small bunch sweet basil (maenglak)
1 chilli ground dried chillies

PREPARATION :

1. Add 2 1/2 cups water to the grated coconut and squeeze out 5 1/2 cups coconut milk. Skim off 1/2 cup coconut cream and set aside to add at the end.
2. Wash and clean the fish, removing head and entrails, and boil until done in 1 cup water. Save the water in which the fish was boiled.
3. Remove the meat from the fish, add to the chilli paste in the mortar, and pound to mix thoroughly. Dip paste into a pot, mix in coconut milk, and heat to boiling. Add the fish broth and fish sauce and simmer, stirring regularly to prevent sticking. When the sauce has thickened and its surface glistens bright red, add the coconut cream and remove from heat.
4. Spoon the hot sauce over the rice vermicelli, vegetables, and egg arranged on plates just before serving.

8 Serving

เครื่องปรุงน้ำพริก

หอมหั่นหยาบ ๆ 7 หัว กระเทียม 2 หัว
ข่า 2 ช้อนชา ตะไคร้ (1 ต้น) 2 ช้อนโต๊ะ
กระชายหั่นละเอียด 1 ถ้วย
พริกแห้งแกะเมล็ดออก 3 เม็ดใหญ่
เกลือ 1 ช้อนชา
กะปิ 1 ช้อนชา
ปลาเค็มปิ้งหนา 1 นิ้ว 1 ชิ้น
น้ำ 1 ถ้วย

เตรียมเครื่องทุกอย่างใส่น้ำตั้งไฟอ่อน เคี่ยวจนนุ่มยกลง บดให้ละเอียด (ก่อนจะบดปล่อยให้เย็นก่อน)

เครื่องปรุงอื่น ๆ

มะพร้าว (หรือกะทิ 5 1/2 ถ้วย) 400 กรัม
ปลาเนื้อ ๆ 1 ตัว 200 กรัม น้ำปลา 2-3 ช้อนโต๊ะ
ไข่ต้ม 15 นาที 2 ฟอง ขนมจีน 1 กิโลกรัม
มะระผ่าครึ่งลูกหั่นบาง ๆ ต้ม 1/2 ลูก
กะหล่ำปลีหั่น 1/2 ถ้วย
ถั่วฝักยาวต้มหั่น 1/2 ถ้วย
แตงหั่น 1/2 ถ้วย
ถั่วงอกลวก 1/2 ถ้วย ใบแมงลัก 1 กำเล็ก พริกแดง 1 เม็ด พริกป่น

วิธีทำ

1. คั้นมะพร้าว ใส่น้ำ 4 1/2 ถ้วย คั้นให้ได้ 5 1/2 ถ้วย ช้อนหัวไว้ 1/2 ถ้วย สำหรับใส่ครั้งสุดท้าย
2. ล้างปลาเอาไส้และหัวออก ต้มในน้ำเดือด 1 ถ้วย ต้มจนสุก เก็บน้ำต้มปลาไว้ แกะเนื้อปลาบดกับพริกและน้ำกะทิตั้งไฟอ่อน ๆ ให้เดือดใส่น้ำต้มปลา ใส่น้ำปลา เคี่ยวไปเรื่อย ๆ หมั่นคนอย่าให้ติดก้นหม้อ พอขันหอมและสีน้ำยาออกสีแดง ๆ ลอยหน้า ใส่หัวกะทิปล่อยให้เดือดอีกครั้ง ยกลง
3. จัดขนมจีน และผักวางข้าง ๆ และไข่ ราดด้วยน้ำยา

KHANOM JIN NAM PHRIK
(Vermicelli and Prawn Sauce)
ขนมจีนน้ำพริก

INGREDIENTS FOR SPICE MIXTURE :

2 tbsp. roasted shallot
2 tbsp. roasted garlic   1 tsp. roasted galangal
1 tbsp. chopped coriander root
1 tbsp. ground dried chilli

OTHER INGREDIENTS :

400 grams grated coconut or 3 3/4 cups coconut milk
400 grams prawns, shelled and deveined
50 grams ground roasted shelled mungbean
2 tbsp. chopped garlic 7 dried small chillies
1/4 cup cooking oil 6 tbsp. fish sauce
6 tbsp. palm sugar 6 tbsp. lemon juice
400 grams vermicelli
1/2 cups boiled swamp cabbage, sliced
1/2 cup boiled yard long bean, sliced
1/2 cup sliced banana flower, soaked in lemon juice befor served
1/4 cup fried dried chillies.

PREPARATION :

1. Pound the roasted garlic, shallot, galangal, the coriander root in a mortar until well ground and thoroughly mixed.

2. Add 2 1/2 cups warm water to the grated coconut and squeeze out 3 3/4 cups coconut milk. Skim off 1 cup coconut cream. Place coconut cream in a pot and heat until some oil surfaces, remove from heat and set aside.

3. Heat 1 cup of the remaining coconut milk and 1 cup of water to boiling, and add the prawns. When the prawns are done, remove them from the pot, place them in a mortar, and pound well.

4. Add the remaining 1 3/4 cups of coconut to the pot in which the prawns were cooked. Add, a little at a time and stirring after each addition, the spice mixture along with the pounded prawns. Then, mix in the mungbeans and add the fish sauce, palm sugar, and lime juice to give the sauce a sour, sweet, and salty taste. When satisfied, remove the pot from the heat.

5. Sauté the chopped garlic in the cooking oil. When it begins to brown, remove the garlic from the oil, put the ground dried chilli in, and reduce the heat.

6. When the oil has taken on a red color, transfer it to the pot containing the sauce, add the coconut milk set aside earlier, and sprinkle with the sautééd garlic.

7. To serve, place four coils of vermicelli on each plate, add all vegetables, and then spoon on about 1/2 cup of the sauce.

5-6 Serving

เครื่องปรุงน้ำพริก

หอมเผา 2 ช้อนโต๊ะ
กระเทียมเผา 2 ช้อนโต๊ะ ข่าเผา 1 ช้อนชา
รากผักชีหั่นละเอียด 1 ช้อนโต๊ะ
พริกป่น 1 ช้อนโต๊ะ

เครื่องปรุงอื่น ๆ

มะพร้าวขูดกระต่ายจีน 500 กรัม (หรือกะทิ 3 3/4 ถ้วย)
กุ้งแกะเปลือก ชักเส้นดำ 400 กรัม
ถั่วทองคั่วบด 2 กรัม กระเทียมสับ 2 ช้อนโต๊ะ
พริกแห้งเม็ดเล็ก 7 เม็ด น้ำมันพืช 1/4 ถ้วย
น้ำปลา 6 ช้อนโต๊ะ น้ำตาลปีบ 6 ช้อนโต๊ะ
น้ำมะนาว 6 ช้อนโต๊ะ ขนมจีน 40 กรัม
ผักบุ้งต้มหั่น 1/2 ถ้วย
ถั่วฝักยาวต้มหั่น 1/2 ถ้วย
หัวปลีอ่อนหั่นบาง (แช่น้ำมะนาวก่อนเสิร์ฟ) 1/2 ถ้วย
พริกแห้งทอด 1/4 ถ้วย

วิธีทำ

1. คั้นมะพร้าวใส่น้ำ 2 1/2 ถ้วย คั้นให้ได้กะทิ 3 3/4 ถ้วย ช้อนหัวกะทิไว้ 1 ถ้วย โขลกหอมเผากระเทียมเผา ข่า รากผักชี ให้ละเอียด

2. เคี่ยวหัวกะทิให้แตกมันมาก ๆ ยกลงพักไว้ก่อน

3. ต้มกุ้งกับหางกะทิที่เหลือให้สุก ตักกุ้งขึ้นโขลกให้ละเอียด

4. ผสมหัวกะทิและหางรวมกัน ใส่กะทิผสมลงในกุ้งทีละน้อย ใส่ถั่วป่น ใส่น้ำพริกที่โขลกและน้ำปลา น้ำตาล ชิมรสเปรี้ยวเค็มหวาน

5. เจียวกระเทียมในน้ำมันพืชหรือขี้โล้ พอเหลืองตักขึ้น เจียวพริกป่นต่อ (ไฟอ่อน) พอน้ำมันเป็นสีแดง ตักใส่หม้อน้ำพริกใส่ผักชีกระเทียมเจียว

KHAO PHAT MU KUNG SAI KHAI
(Fried Rice with Pork, Shrimp and Egg)
ข้าวผัดหมู กุ้ง ใส่ไข่

INGREDIENTS :

4 cups cooked rice
150 grams pork
150 grams shrimp, shelled and deveined
2 eggs
1/4 cup cooking oil
1 onion
2 tbsp. catsup
1 tbsp. sugar
3 tbsp. light soy sauce
1/2 head cabbage
1 spur chilli, sliced
2 cucumbers
6 spring onions
1 lettuce
1 lime

PREPARATION :

1. Cut the pork into small pieces and marinate in 1 tbsp. light soy sauce for a few minutes.

2. Cut the onion into slices about 1/5 inch thick.

3. Heat the oil in a wok; when the oil is hot, fry the onions and then the pork, shrimp, catsup, sugar, and soy sauce. Fry with stirring until the pork is done and then add the rice. Continue stirring the rice, scraping the bottom of the wok regularly to guard against sticking, until the desired degree of dryness is reached; then, spoon the rice from the wok.

4. Return the wok to the heat, add 1 tbsp. of oil, allow it to heat and then break the eggs into the wok. With the spatula, break, spread, and turn the eggs and when done, cut into strips. Add the fried rice, and mix well.

5. Put the fried rice on a plate, shreds of chilli, and serve with cucumber, spring onions, cabbage, lettuce and wedges of lime.

4 Serving

เครื่องปรุง

ข้าวสุก 4 ถ้วย
หมู 150 กรัม
กุ้งแกะเปลือกชักเส้นดำ 150 กรัม
ไข่ไก่ 2 ฟอง น้ำมันพืช 1/4 ถ้วย
หอมใหญ่ 1 หัว ซอสมะเขือเทศ 2 ช้อนโต๊ะ
น้ำตาลทราย 1 ช้อนโต๊ะ
ซีอิ๊วขาว 3 ช้อนโต๊ะ
กะหล่ำปลี 1/2 หัว
พริกแดง 1 เม็ด แตงกวา 2 ผล
ต้นหอม 6 ต้น ผักกาดหอม 1 ต้น
มะนาวหั่นเป็นชิ้น 1 ลูก

วิธีทำ

1. หั่นหมูเป็นชิ้นเล็ก หมักกับซีอิ๊วขาว 1 ช้อนโต๊ะไว้สักพักหนึ่ง

2. หั่นหัวหอมเป็นชิ้นหนาประมาณ 1/5 นิ้ว

3. ใส่น้ำมันในกระทะตั้งไฟ เมื่อน้ำมันร้อนใส่หัวหอม หมู กุ้ง ลงผัดกับซอสมะเขือเทศ น้ำตาลทราย และซีอิ๊ว เมื่อหมูสุกจึงใส่ข้าวลงผัดจนข้าวดูแห้งดี จึงตักขึ้น

4. ใส่น้ำมันลงในกระทะ 1 ช้อนโต๊ะ เมื่อน้ำมันร้อนใส่ไข่ดีเข้ากัน เจียวจนไข่สุก ใช้ตะหลิวสับให้เป็นชิ้นเล็ก ๆ เทข้าวใส่กระทะคนพอทั่ว ตักข้าวใส่จานแบ่ง 4 จาน

5. โรยผักชีและพริกชอย เสิร์ฟกับแตงกวา ต้นหอม กะหล่ำปลี ผักกาดหอม และมะนาว

PHAT THAI SAI KHAI
(Fried Noodles Thai Style)
ผัดไทยใส่ไข่

INGREDIENTS :

300 grams narrow rice noodles
1/2 kg bean sprouts
3 eggs
50 grams pork, cut into small slivers
50 grams chopped pickled white radish
1 cake soybean curd, cut into small slivers
1/2 cup ground roasted peanuts
1 tsp. ground dried chillies
1 tbsp. chopped shallots
1 tbsp. chopped garlic
1/2 cup cooking oil
4 tbsp. sugar
3 tbsp. fish sauce
4 tbsp. tamaind juice or vinegar
50 grams Chinese leek leaves
1/2 banana blassom

PREPARATION :

1. Heat 3 tbsp. oil in a frying pan and sauté garlic and shallots. When yellowed, add noodles with just enough water to soften them and fry, turning constantly with spatula to prevent sticking. Then move noodles to side of pan or remove from pan.

2. Put 3 tbsp. oil into pan. When hot, fry the pork, pickled white radish, bean curd, and dried chillies and then return the noodles, mix thoroughly, and move to the plat.

3. Put 2 tbsp. oil into the pan. When heated, break 3 eggs into pan and scramble with spatula, spreading egg in a thin layer over the pan. When set, return the noodles and mix together. Add half the bean sprouts and the Chinese leek leaves and turn to mix together. Spoon onto plates and sprinkle with ground peanut. Serve with bean sprouts, banana blassom, Chinese leek, and Indian pennywort.

Fried noodles require a lot of oil; however, it is possible to use less than indicated above by adding small amounts from time to time to keep the noodles from drying instead of adding all the oil at once.

> 3 Serving

เครื่องปรุง

ก๋วยเตี๋ยวเส้นเล็ก 300 กรัม ถั่วงอก 1/2 กิโลกรัม
ไข่ 3 ฟอง
เนื้อหมูหั่นเล็กๆ 50 กรัม หัวผักกาดเค็มสับ 50 กรัม
เต้าหู้หั่นเล็กๆ 1 แผ่น ถั่วลิสงป่น 1/2 ถ้วย
พริกป่น 1 ช้อนชา หอมสับ 1 ช้อนโต๊ะ
กระเทียมสับ 1 ช้อนโต๊ะ น้ำมัน 1/2 ถ้วย
น้ำตาล 4 ช้อนโต๊ะ น้ำปลา 3 ช้อนโต๊ะ
ส้มมะขามหรือน้ำส้ม 4 ช้อนโต๊ะ
ใบกุยช่าย 50 กรัม มะนาว 1 ผลใหญ่
หัวปลี 1 ซีก

วิธีทำ

1. เจียวหอม กระเทียมกับน้ำมัน 3 ช้อนโต๊ะ ใส่เส้น ใส่น้ำเล็กน้อยพอให้เส้นนุ่ม ปรุงรสผัดให้เข้ากันเร็วๆ อย่าให้เส้นเกาะกันเป็นก้อน กันเส้นไว้ข้างกระทะหรือตักขึ้น

2. ใส่น้ำมัน 3 ช้อนโต๊ะ ผัดเนื้อหมู ผักกาดเค็ม เต้าหู้ พริกป่น ตลบเส้นลงมาคลุกให้เข้ากัน กันเส้นไว้ข้างกระทะ

3. ใส่น้ำมัน 2 ช้อนโต๊ะ ต่อยไข่ใส่ กระจายบางๆ แล้วกลับเส้นลงผัด ใส่ถั่วงอกครึ่งหนึ่ง ใส่ใบกุยช่ายตักขึ้น โรยถั่วลิสง รับประทานกับผัก เช่น ถั่วงอก หัวปลี ต้นกุยช่าย ใบบัวบก
หมายเหตุ ผัดไทยใช้น้ำมันมาก แต่ไม่ใส่ครั้งเดียวควรใช้เติมในขณะที่เส้นแห้ง อาจจะไม่ต้องหมดตามส่วนที่ให้ก็ได้

SEN JAN PHAT KUNG
(Stir-Fried Rice Noodles and Prawns)
เส้นจันทน์ผัดกุ้ง

INGREDIENTS :

4 cups dried narrow rice noodles (Chanthaburi noodles), soaked about 5 minutes in water
8-10 prawns shelled and deveined
2 tbsp. chopped garlic
2 tbsp. cup shallots
5 dried chillies, seeds removed, soaked in water
1/4 tsp. salt
1/4 cup cooking oil
1/4 cup palm sugar
1/4 cup tamarind juice
1/4 cup fish sauce
50 grams bean sprouts
100 grams Chinese chives cut into short leangths
2-3 limes

PREPARATION :

1. Peel the garlic and shallots and slice dried chillies. Place the chilli and the salt in a mortar and pound, then add the garlic and shallots and pound until ground and mixed thoroughly.

2. Heat the oil in a wok. When hot, fry the pounded chilli paste, add sugar, tamarind juice and fish sauce to taste. Then add the prawns and stir, turning regularly until done.

3. Add the noodles, turning for a few minutes. Then, add the bean sprouts, and Chinese chives and mix.

4. Serve with Chinese chives, bean sprouts and wedges of lime.

4 Serving

เครื่องปรุง

ก๋วยเตี๋ยวเส้นเล็ก (เส้นจันทน์) แช่น้ำประมาณ 5 นาที 4 ถ้วย
กุ้งแกะเปลือก ชักเส้นดำ 8-10 ตัว
กระเทียมสับ 2 ช้อนโต๊ะ
หอมแดงซอย 2 ช้อนโต๊ะ
พริกแห้ง แกะเม็ดออก แช่น้ำ 5 เม็ด
เกลือป่น 1/4 ช้อนชา น้ำมันพืช 1/4 ถ้วย
น้ำตาลปีบ 1/4 ถ้วย น้ำส้มมะขาม 1/4 ถ้วย
น้ำปลา 1/4 ถ้วย
ถั่วงอก 50 กรัม
กุยช่ายตัดเป็นท่อนสั้น 100 กรัม
มะนาว หั่นเป็นชิ้น 2-3 ผล

วิธีทำ

1. ปอกกระเทียม หัวหอมและหั่นพริกแห้งเป็นชิ้นเล็ก โขลกพริกกับเกลือป่น แล้วจึงใส่กระเทียมกับหัวหอมลงโขลกให้แหลกเข้ากัน

2. ใส่น้ำมันในกระทะ ตั้งไฟ เมื่อน้ำมันร้อน ตักกระเทียม หัวหอม และพริกโขลกลงเจียวให้หอม ปรุงรสน้ำตาล น้ำส้มมะขาม น้ำปลา ก่อนใส่กุ้งลงผัดให้สุก

3. ใส่เส้นลงผัดสักครู่ จึงใส่ถั่วงอกกับกุยช่ายลงผัดด้วยแล้วตักขึ้น

4. เสิร์ฟกับหัวปลี กุยช่าย ถั่วงอก แดง ถั่ว และมะนาว

KHAO KLUK KAPI
(Fried Rice and Shrimp Paste)
ข้าวคลุกกะปิ

INGREDIENTS :

3 cups cooked rice
1 tbsp. minced garlic
1 tbsp. shrimp paste
1 tbsp. water
1 tsp. sugar
1 tbsp. fish sauce
4 tbsp. shallots sliced thin
1 egg
1/2 cup cooking oil
3 tbsp. fried dried shrimp
1 coriander plant, coarsely chopped
1 red chilli sliced thin
1 lettuce
2 limes

PREPARATION :

1. Fry the garlic in a wok, mix 1 tbsp. water with the shrimp paste and add to the pan. Add the sugar and fish sauce and reduce the heat.

2. Add the rice and stir to mix well, then remove from the wok.

3. Beat the egg. Place 1 tbsp. oil in a wok and heat. When the wok is hot, spread the oil, pour in the egg, and spread it in a thin layer over the wok. When set well, remove from the wok, roll up, and cut into thin slices.

4. Dip portions of the rice onto plates, add egg, sweet pork, dried shrimp and shallots. Serve with lettuce, spring onion, wedges of lime and chilli.

INGREDIENTS FOR SWEET PORK :

1 cup pork, thinly sliced
2 tbsp. palm sugar
1 tbsp. chopped garlic
1 tbsp. fish sauce
1 tsp. dark soy sauce
2 tbsp. cooking oil   1/4 cup water

PREPARATION :

1. Mix the pork and the garlic. Fry the pork in the cooking oil until the pork is just done.

2. Add the fish sauce, dark soy sauce and sugar, stirring regularly. Add the water. Cover the wok and simmer until the water is dried. Remove from heat.

3 Serving

เครื่องปรุง

ข้าวสุก 3 ถ้วย
กระเทียมสับ 1 ช้อนโต๊ะ
กะปิ 1 ช้อนโต๊ะ น้ำ 1 ช้อนโต๊ะ
น้ำตาล 1 ช้อนชา น้ำปลา 1 ช้อนโต๊ะ
หอมแดงซอย 4 ช้อนโต๊ะ ไข่ไก่ 1 ฟอง
น้ำมันพืช 1/2 ถ้วย
กุ้งแห้งทอดกรอบ 3 ช้อนโต๊ะ
ผักชีหั่นหยาบ 1 ต้น
พริกแดงซอยละเอียด 1 เม็ด
ผักกาดหอม 1 ต้น
มะนาวฝานเป็นชิ้น 2 ผล

วิธีทำ

1. เจียวกระเทียมให้หอม ละลายกะปิกับน้ำ 1 ช้อนโต๊ะ แล้วใส่ลงกระทะ เติมน้ำตาล น้ำปลา หรี่ไฟลง

2. ใส่ข้าวลงผัดให้เข้ากัน สักครู่ตักขึ้น

3. ตีไข่ ใส่น้ำมัน 1 ช้อนโต๊ะในกระทะ ตั้งไฟให้กระทะร้อน กลอกกระทะ คนให้น้ำมันแผ่ทั่วก้นกระทะแล้วเทไข่ลงไปกลอกเป็นแผ่นบางพอสุกตักขึ้น วางบนเขียง ม้วนแผ่นไข่แล้วหั่นขวางเป็นเส้นฝอย

4. ตักข้าวใส่จานเสิร์ฟ ใส่ไข่ หมูหวาน กุ้งแห้งทอด และหอมซอย เสิร์ฟ กับผักกาดหอม ต้นหอม มะนาว และพริก มะนาวหั่นเป็นเสี้ยวหรือใช้ แอปเปิ้ลเปรี้ยวหรือมะม่วงสับเป็นชิ้นเล็ก ๆ แทนมะนาว

วิธีทำหมูหวาน

เจียวกระเทียมสับ 1 ช้อนโต๊ะในน้ำมันพืช 2 ช้อนโต๊ะให้หอม ใส่หมูหั่น เป็นชิ้นเล็ก 1 ถ้วย ผัดพอสุก เติมน้ำปลา 1 ช้อนโต๊ะ ซีอิ๊วหวาน 1 ช้อนชา และน้ำตาลปีบ 2 ช้อนโต๊ะ หมั่นคนไปมา เติมน้ำ 1/4 ถ้วย ปิดฝาตั้งไฟอ่อน จนน้ำแห้งตักขึ้น

KHAO OP KUN CHIANG
(Chinese Sausage Steamed in Rice)
ข้าวอบกุนเชียง

INGREDIENTS :

2 cups milled rice
2 Chinese sausages (kun chiang)
100 grams lean pork
200 grams small prawns
3 Shiitake mushrooms, soaked in water
2 tbsp. oyster sauce
2 tbsp. light soy sauce
10 cloves garlic, chopped
4 tbsp. cooking oil
1/4 cup sliced thin ginger root,

PREPARATION :

1. Slice the sausage. Cut the pork into small thin strips. Shell and clean the prawns.

2. After the mushrooms have absorbed water and filled out, cut them into thin slices. Save the water in which the mushrooms were soaked.

3. Wash and drain the rice.

4. Place the oil in a wok over medium heat. When it is hot, put in the garlic and ginger and fry with regular stirring long enough for the flavors to come out; then, add the sausage, pork, prawns, and mushroom. Stir, and then add the rice, the oyster sauce and soy sauce. Work with the spatula until all the ingredients are thoroughly mixed; then, transfer the mixture to a pot.

5. Add enough water to the water in which the mushrooms were soaked to obtain a total of three cups, add this to the pot, and then place the pot on the heat.

6. Cooking time is about 30-35 minutes. Toward the end, cover the pot and reduce the heat. When the rice is done, remove from the heat and allow the rice to stand for a time in the covered pot. Spoon onto plates and serve with pineapple or fresh vegetables, such as cabbage and spring onions.

4 Serving

เครื่องปรุง

ข้าวสาร 2 ถ้วย
กุนเชียง 2 อัน
หมูเนื้อสัน 100 กรัม
กุ้ง 200 กรัม เห็ดหอม แช่น้ำ 3 ดอก
ซอสน้ำมันหอย 2 ช้อนโต๊ะ ซีอิ๊วขาว 2 ช้อนโต๊ะ
กระเทียมสับ 10 กลีบ น้ำมันพืช 4 ช้อนโต๊ะ
ขิงหั่นบาง ๆ 1/4 ถ้วย

วิธีทำ

1. หั่นกุนเชียง และหมู แกะเปลือกกุ้ง ชักเส้นดำออก

2. เมื่อเห็ดหอมนุ่มแล้ว หั่นเป็นชิ้นบาง เก็บน้ำที่แช่เห็ดเอาไว้

3. ซาวข้าว

4. ใส่น้ำมันในกระทะ ตั้งไฟแรงปานกลางให้น้ำมันร้อน ใส่กระเทียมกับขิง ลงผัดจนหอม ใส่กุนเชียง หมู กุ้งลงผัด พอสุกใส่เห็ดแล้วใส่ข้าว ปรุงรส ด้วยซอสน้ำมันหอยและซีอิ๊ว ผัดคลุกให้เครื่องปรุงเข้ากันดี ตักใส่หม้อ

5. เติมน้ำลงในน้ำแช่เห็ดหอมให้ได้ปริมาณ 3 ถ้วย ใส่น้ำนี้ลงในหม้อ ตั้งไฟ ประมาณ 30-35 นาที ในตอนท้ายปิดฝาหม้อ หรี่ไฟลง เมื่อข้าวสุกยกลง พักไว้โดยไม่เปิดฝาหม้อพักใหญ่ แล้วจึงตักใส่จาน เสิร์ฟกับสับปะรดหรือ ผักสด เช่นกะหล่ำปลีและต้นหอม

KHAO RAT NA KAI
(Chicken in Sauce on Rice)
ข้าวราดหน้าไก่

INGREDIENTS :

4 cups cooked rice
400 grams chicken
100 grams chicken livers
1 onion
1/2 cup pineapple, cut into small pieces
1/2 cup straw mushrooms
1/2 cub tomatoes, cut into bite-sized pieces
150 grams Chinese mustrad green (phak kwangtung) cut into 1 inch lengths
100 grams spring onions cut into 1 inch lengths
3 tbsp. light soy sauce
2 1/2 cup chicken stock
3 tbsp. tapioca flour mixed in 1/4 cup water
1 tsp. sugar
1/2 tsp. pepper
1 tbsp. chopped garlic
2 tbsp. cooking oil
3 sliced chillies
1/4 cup vinegar

PREPARATION :

1. Cut the chicken meat and livers into small slices and marinate in 1 tbsp. light soy sauce.

2. Peel and wash onion, cut in half, then cut across into thin slices

3. Heat oil in a wok, brown the garlic, then add the chicken meat and livers and fry until done. Add the onion slices. When cooked, add the mushrooms, pineapple, tomato, mustard green, and hot chicken stock. Add light soy sauce and sugar to taste and thicken with the tapioca flour in water. When boiling, taste and season as necessary, then add the spring onion and remove from heat.

4. Spoon about 1 cup cooked rice on a serving plate, and top with the hot chicken in sauce, sprinkle with pepper, and serve immediately.

5. Serve with the chilli cut into thin rings in vinegar.

3 Serving

เครื่องปรุง

ข้าวสุก 4 ถ้วย
เนื้อไก่ 400 กรัม ตับไก่ 100 กรัม
หอมใหญ่ 1 หัว
สับปะรดหั่นชิ้นพอคำ 1/2 ถ้วย
เห็ดฟางหรือเห็ดซองปี๊บองผ่าครึ่ง 1/2 ถ้วย
มะเขือเทศผลใหญ่หั่นเป็นชิ้นพอคำ 1/2 ถ้วย
ผักกวางตุ้งหั่นเป็นท่อนยาว 1 นิ้ว 150 กรัม
ต้นหอมหั่นเป็นท่อนยาว 1 นิ้ว 100 กรัม
ซีอิ๊วขาว 3 ช้อนโต๊ะ น้ำต้มกระดูก 2 1/2 ถ้วย
แป้งมันสำปะหลัง 3 ช้อนโต๊ะ ละลายในน้ำ 1/4 ถ้วย
น้ำตาลทราย 1 ช้อนชา พริกไทย 1/2 ช้อนชา
กระเทียมสับ 1 ช้อนโต๊ะ น้ำมันพืช 2 ช้อนโต๊ะ
พริกชี้ฟ้าหั่น 3 เม็ด น้ำส้มสายชู 1/4 ถ้วย

วิธีทำ

1. หั่นเนื้อไก่และตับไก่เป็นชิ้นเล็ก หมักกับซีอิ๊วขาว 1 ช้อนโต๊ะ

2. ปอกเปลือกหัวหอม ผ่าครึ่งแล้วหั่นขวางเป็นชิ้นยาว

3. ใส่น้ำมันในกระทะ เจียวกระเทียมแล้วใส่ไก่กับตับลงผัดให้สุก แล้วจึงใส่หัวหอม เห็ด ผักกวางตุ้ง แล้วเติมน้ำต้มกระดูก ปรุงรสด้วยซีอิ๊วและน้ำตาล ใส่สับปะรด ใส่มะเขือเทศ แป้งมันละลายน้ำ พอเดือดชิมและปรุงรสดูอีกครั้งตามต้องการ ใส่ต้นหอม แล้วตักขึ้น

4. แบ่งข้าวเป็น 4 ส่วนใส่บนจาน ตักหน้าไก่ราดข้าวแต่งด้วยพริก โรยพริกไทย

5. เสิร์ฟกับพริกดอง หั่นพริกบาง ๆ แช่ลงในน้ำส้ม

THUA KHIAO TOM NAM TAN
(Mungbeans in Syrup)
ถั่วเขียวต้มน้ำตาล

INGREDIENTS :

1 cup mungbeans
1 cup light brown sugar
5 cups water

PREPARATION :

1. Soak the mungbeans overnight or at least three hours, and then drain.

2. Boil the mungbeans in the 5 cups water until tender and then add the sugar. When the sugar has dissolved completely and the syrup has returned to a strong boil, remove from the heat.

4 Serving

FAK THONG KAENG BUAT
(Pumpkin in Coconut Cream)
ฟักทองแกงบวด

INGREDIENTS :

1 kg. pumpkin
1 cup coconut cream
4 cups coconut milk
1 cup water
3/4 cup palm sugar
1/4 cup sugar
1/2 tsp. salt

PREPARATION :

1. Wash the skin of the pumpkin clean. Remove some, but not all, of the skin; the outer surface need not be completely smooth. Remove the seeds and membrane from the inside and cut the flesh into uniform pieces about one-half inch thick.

2. Take 4 cups of the coconut milk, mix it with the palm sugar, sugar, salt, and the 1 cup water, heat to boiling, add the pumpkin, and continue cooking. When the pumpkin is tender, add the coconut cream, bring to a boil once again, and remove from the heat. Serve in small bowls.

6 Serving

ส่วนผสม

ถั่วเขียว 1 ถ้วย
น้ำตาลทรายแดง 1 ถ้วย น้ำ 5 ถ้วย

วิธีทำ

1. แช่ถั่วเขียวไว้ในน้ำ 3 ชั่วโมง หรือค้างคืนไว้ แล้วสรงขึ้นจากน้ำ

2. ต้มน้ำ 5 ถ้วย ใส่ถั่วเขียวที่แช่ไว้ลงต้มจนนุ่มดีแล้ว ใส่น้ำตาลทรายแดง ลงทั้งหมด พอน้ำตาลละลายดี เดือดทั่วกันก็ใช้ได้

ส่วนผสม

ฟักทอง 1 ก.ก. หัวกะทิ 1 ถ้วย
หางกะทิ 4 ถ้วย น้ำ 1 ถ้วย
น้ำตาลปีบ 3/4 ถ้วย
น้ำตาลทราย 1/4 ถ้วย เกลือ 1/2 ช้อนชา

วิธีทำ

1. ล้างเปลือกฟักทองให้สะอาด ปอกเปลือกเล็กน้อยเหลือส่วนเขียว ๆ ติด บ้างไม่ต้องปอกจนเกลี้ยง คว้านเมล็ดออกหั่นชิ้นหนา 1/2 นิ้ว หั่นให้ชิ้น เท่า ๆ กัน

2. ผสมน้ำตาลปีบ น้ำตาลทราย เกลือ กับหางกะทิใส่หม้อตั้งไฟพอน้ำตาล ละลายกรองใส่หม้อตั้งไฟใหม่พอเดือด ใส่ฟักทองลงต้มจนสุก ราดด้วย หัวกะทิที่แบ่งไว้พอเดือด ยกลง ตักใส่ถ้วยแก้วเสิร์ฟ

KHAO PHOT PIAK
(Corn Pudding with Coconut Cream)
ข้าวโพดเปียก

INGREDIENTS :

3 cups sliced kernels of corn
1 1/2 cups water
1 cup sugar
4 tbsp. tapioca flour or corn flour in 1/2 cup of water
1 cup coconut cream
1/2 tsp. salt

PREPARATION :

1. Heat the water to boiling, add the corn, and boil, stirring constantly, until tender (five minutes).

2. Add the sugar and the flour, stirring all the while, continue cooking. When smooth, remove from the heat.

3. Add salt to the coconut cream, bring to a boil, and then remove from the heat.

4. Place a portion of the corn pudding into individual dessert dishes and top with the coconut cream.

4 Serving

KLUAI BUAT CHI
(Bananas in Coconut Cream)
กล้วยบวชชี

INGREDIENTS :

10 ripe Nam Wa variety bananas
1/2 cup coconut cream
3 cups coconut milk
1 cup sugar 1 tsp. salt

PREPARATION :

1. Peel the bananas and cut into quarters.

2. Place the coconut milk in a pot and heat to boiling. Add the bananas and cook over a medium heat until tender; then, add the sugar and salt; stir until dissolved.

3. Add the coconut cream, spoon into bowls, and, serve.

Khai-variety bananas may also be used.

If the bananas are very ripe, reduce the amount of sugar used. If the bananas are not yet fully ripe, they may not be sweet and may have a certain astringency. If so, first boil the bananas in plain water. Remove them from the water, and then proceed as in the above recipe except that the sugar should be dissolved in the coconut milk before the bananas are added. This will reduce the astringency and give the bananas and coconut cream a more appetizing appearance.

5 Serving

ส่วนผสม

ข้าวโพดฝานบางๆ 3 ถ้วย น้ำ 2 ถ้วย
น้ำตาลทราย 1 ถ้วย แป้งมันหรือแป้งข้าวโพด 4 ช้อนโต๊ะ
หัวกะทิ 1 ถ้วย เกลือ 1/2 ช้อนชา

วิธีทำ

1. ต้มน้ำให้เดือด ใส่ข้าวโพดลงต้ม หมั่นคน ต้มพอสุกประมาณ 5 นาที

2. เติมน้ำตาล ละลายแป้งมันใส่ หมั่นคน พอแป้งสุกยกลง

3. ใส่เกลือลงในหัวกะทิ ตั้งไฟจนเดือด แล้วยกลง

4. เสิร์ฟ ตักข้าวโพดเปียกใส่ถ้วย แล้วราดหน้าด้วยน้ำกะทิ

ส่วนผสม

กล้วยน้ำว้าสุกกำลังดี 10 ผล
กะทิส่วนหัว 1/2 ถ้วย ส่วนหางกะทิ 3 ถ้วย
น้ำตาลทราย 1 ถ้วย เกลือ 1 ช้อนชา

วิธีทำ

1. ปอกเปลือกกล้วย ผ่าครึ่งลูก แล้วจึงตัดครึ่ง

2. ใส่กะทิลงในหม้อตั้งไฟพอเดือด ใส่กล้วยตั้งไฟต่อ ใช้ไฟกลางพอกล้วยสุก ใส่น้ำตาลและเกลือพอน้ำตาลละลายและร้อนทั่ว

3. ใส่หัวกะทิลงกลาง ตักใส่ถ้วยเสิร์ฟ

THUA DAM KAENG BUAT
(Black Beans in Coconut Cream)

ถั่วดำแกงบวด

INGREDIENTS:

1 cup black beans
2 1/2 cups coconut milk
1 cup palm sugar
1/4 tsp. salt

PREPARATION:

1. Soak the beans three hours (or leave them soaking overnight), boil them in the water in which they were soaked, and when they are tender, remove from the heat and drain off the water.

2. Mix the coconut milk with the salt and sugar until the salt and sugar has dissolved; then, bring to a boil, filter through cheesecloth, and then return to the heat.

3. Add the beans, and when the coconut cream has returned to a good boil, remove from the heat.

KHANOM BUA LOI THUA KHIAO
(Mungbean Balls in Coconut Cream)

ขนมบัวลอยถั่วเขียว

INGREDIENTS:

1/3 cup hulled mungbeans
2 cups coconut milk
1/2 cup palm sugar
1/2 cup glutinous rice flour
1/4 cup water   1/4 tsp. salt

PREPARATION:

1. Soak the mungbeans in water for 1 1/2 hours; next, remove them from the water and steam them until tender; then, mash them to a fine paste.

2. Set aside one cup of the coconut milk. Mix the remainder with the palm sugar and salt in a pot, bring to a boil, stirring regularly to prevent lumps from forming, and then remove from the heat.

3. Mix the mashed mungbeans with the glutinous rice flour. adding a little water (no more than 1/4 cup) a little at a time and kneading to obtain a soft dough. Roll the dough into balls about 1/4 inch in diameter. Cook the balls by placing in boiling water; when the balls float to the surface, remove them from the water and put them into the pot of boiled coconut milk.

4. Place the pot on the heat once again, add the cup of coconut milk set aside earlier, and remove from the heat, and dip into small bowls to serve.

ส่วนผสม

ถั่วดำดิบ 1 ถ้วย
กะทิ 2 1/2 ถ้วย
น้ำตาลมะพร้าวหรือน้ำตาลโตนด 1 ถ้วย
เกลือ 1/4 ช้อนชา

วิธีทำ

1. แช่ถั่วดำ 3 ชั่วโมง หรือค้างคืนต้มให้สุกเปื่อย รินน้ำออก

2. ผสมกะทิ เกลือและน้ำตาล คนให้ละลาย ยกขึ้นตั้งไฟพอเดือด กรอง ด้วยผ้าขาวบางแล้วต้มอีกครั้ง

3. ใส่ถั่วที่ต้มลงพอเดือดทั่วยกลงใช้ได้

หมายเหตุ กะทิกับน้ำตาลละลายดีแล้วไม่กรองก็ได้

ส่วนผสม

ถั่วเขียวเลาะเปลือก 1/3 ถ้วย กะทิ 2 ถ้วย
น้ำตาลปีบ 1/2 ถ้วย แป้งข้าวเหนียว 1/2 ถ้วย
น้ำนวดแป้ง 1/4 ถ้วย เกลือ 1/4 ช้อนชา

วิธีทำ

1. แช่ถั่วเขียว 1 1/2 ชั่วโมง นึ่งให้สุก บดให้ละเอียด

2. แบ่งกะทิไว้ 1 ถ้วย ผสมกะทิที่เหลือกับน้ำตาลปีบ เกลือ นำไปตั้งไฟ พอเดือด (หมั่นคนอย่าให้เป็นลูก) แล้วยกลง

3. ผสมแป้งกับถั่วบด ใส่น้ำทีละน้อย นวดจนนุ่มปั้นได้ ปั้นเป็นก้อนกลมเล็ก ขนาดเส้นผ่าศูนย์กลาง 1/4 นิ้ว ต้มในน้ำเดือด พอลอยตัวตักขึ้นใส่ในหม้อ กะทิยกขึ้นตั้งไฟใส่หัวกะทิที่เก็บไว้ ยกลง

LOT CHONG SINGKHAPO
(Mungbean Strands in Coconut Syrup)
ลอดช่องสิงคโปร์

INGREDIENTS FOR MUNGBEAN STRANDS:

1/2 cup hulled mungbeans
1 cup tapioca flour   1/4 cup boiling water
2 tbsp. thick pandanus-leaf juice or 1/4 tsp. green food coloring

COCONUT SYRUP

1/2 cup jasmine water   1 cup sugar   1 cup coconut milk

PREPARATION :

1. Soak the mungbeans in water for 1 1/2 hours. Then, boil until tender and mash to a smooth paste.
2. Mix the mashed mungbean with the tapioca flour. Add the boiling water and the pandanus juice (or food coloring) and mix with a wooden paddle. While still warm yet cool enough to work with the hands, knead into a soft, sticky dough. Roll out the dough into thin sheet and cut into strands.
3. Place the strands in boiling water. When they float to the surface, remove them from the hot water, immerse briefly in cold water, and then place in a strainer to drain, pour to coconut syrup, serves with ice.
4. Coconut syrup. Boil the sugar and jasmine water for 5 minutes to make syrup, allow to cool, then add coconut milk.

THABTHIM GROB
(Mock Pomegranate Seeds)
ทับทิมกรอบ

INGREDIENTS:

1 cup diced boiled water chestnuts (30 grams or 40 fresh water chestnuts)
1/2 cup tapioca flour
150 grams sugar
3/4 cup water (for syrup)
3/4 cup coconut milk
red food coloring
crushed ice

PREPARATION:

1. Place red food coloring in a little water and soak the water chestnuts until colored. Remove and place in the flour so the pieces become well coated. Then place these "pomegranate seeds" in a strainer to allow excess flour to fall away.
2. Heat 5 cups water to boiling, boil the pomegranate seeds 3 minutes, remove, place in cold water, remove, drain and wrap in a thin white cloth.
3. Boil the sugar and the water to make syrup, allow to cool, then add the coconut milk.
4. When serving, place the pomegranate seeds in dessert dishes and the syrup and ice.

ส่วนผสม

ถั่วเขียวเลาะเปลือก 1/2 ถ้วย
แป้งมัน 1 ถ้วย น้ำร้อนเดือด 1/4 ถ้วย
น้ำใบเตยข้นๆ 2 ช้อนโต๊ะ หรือสีเขียวใส่อาหาร 1/4 ช้อนชา

ส่วนผสมน้ำเชื่อมกะทิ

น้ำลอยดอกมะลิ 1/2 ถ้วย   น้ำตาลทราย 1 ถ้วย   น้ำกะทิ 1 ถ้วย

วิธีทำ

1. แช่ถั่วเขียว 1 1/2 ชั่วโมง ต้มให้สุก บดให้ละเอียด
2. ผสมถั่วเขียวกับแป้งมัน ใส่น้ำใบเตยและน้ำต้มเดือด ใช้พายคนให้เข้ากัน แล้วนวดแป้งให้เหนียวนุ่ม คลึงแป้งด้วยไม้นวด แผ่ออกเป็นแผ่นบาง ตัดเป็นเส้นๆ
3. ต้มน้ำให้เดือด ใส่แป้งเส้นลงต้ม พอลอยตัวช้อนขึ้น ผ่านน้ำเย็น ใส่ตะแกรงทิ้งให้สะเด็ดน้ำ เทลอดช่องใส่น้ำเชื่อมกะทิ เสิร์ฟกับน้ำแข็ง
4. น้ำเชื่อมกะทิ ต้มน้ำตาลกับน้ำลอยดอกมะลิ 5 นาที ปล่อยให้เย็นผสมน้ำกะทิ

ส่วนผสม

แห้วต้มหั่นสี่เหลี่ยมเล็กๆ 1 ถ้วย
(ถ้าแห้วดิบ 300 กรัมได้ 40 เม็ด)
แป้งมัน 1/2 ถ้วย น้ำตาลทราย 150 กรัม
น้ำทำน้ำเชื่อม 3/4 ถ้วย กะทิ 3/4 ถ้วย
สีขนมสีแดง
น้ำแข็ง

วิธีทำ

1. ละลายสีแดงกับน้ำเล็กน้อย แช่แห้วพอติดสีตักขึ้นคลุกแป้งให้ติดมากๆ ใส่กระชอนร่อน ให้แป้งร่วง
2. ต้มน้ำ 5 ถ้วยให้เดือด ลวกเม็ดทับทิมพอลอย 3 นาที ตักขึ้นใส่น้ำเย็น ตักใส่ผ้าขาวบางไว้
3. คั้นมะพร้าวใส่น้ำ 1/4 ถ้วย คั้นให้ได้ 3/4 ถ้วย
4. ผสมน้ำเชื่อมกับกะทิ เวลารับประทานตักใส่ในถ้วยเม็ดทับทิมใส่น้ำแข็ง

TA-KO SA-KHU
(Sweet Tapioca with Coconut Cream)
ตะโก้สาคู

INGREDIENTS :

2 1/2 cups small tapioca pearls
3 1/4 cups water
1 cup sugar

TOPPING :

2 cups coconut cream
2 tsp. sugar
1/4 cup rice flour
1 tsp. salt

PREPARATION :

1. Wash and drain the tapioca pearls; transfer to a pot, add the sugar and water; boil about 20 minutes until done.

2. Spoon the tapioca into individual the banana leaf cups or small bowls and top with a few spoonfuls of the coconut cream mixture.

TOPPING :

Mix together the coconut cream, salt, sugar and rice flour in another pot, place over medium-low heat and cook until the mixture thickens.

4 Serving

ส่วนผสม

สาคูเม็ดเล็ก 2 1/2 ถ้วย
น้ำ 3 1/4 ถ้วย   น้ำตาล 1 ถ้วย

ส่วนผสมหน้าตะโก้

หัวกะทิ 2 ถ้วย   น้ำตาล 2 ช้อนชา
แป้งข้าวเจ้า 1/4 ถ้วย   เกลือป่น 1 ช้อนชา

วิธีทำ

1. ล้างสาคู สรงขึ้นมาให้สะเด็ดน้ำ ใส่หม้อเติมน้ำและน้ำตาล ตั้งไฟต้มไปประมาณ 20 นาที จนสุก

2. ตักสาคูใส่ในถ้วย ราดหน้าด้วยหัวกะทิประมาณ 3 ช้อนชา

วิธีทำหน้าตะโก้

ผสมหัวกะทิ เกลือป่น น้ำตาลและแป้งข้าวเจ้า คนให้เข้ากันในหม้อ ยกขึ้นตั้งไฟกลางค่อนข้างต่ำ จนส่วนผสมข้น ปิดไฟยกลง

KHANOM MO KAENG PHEUAK
(Taro Coconut Custard)
ขนมหม้อแกงเผือก

INGREDIENTS :

1 1/2 cups mashed boiled taro
1 1/4 cups coconut milk
5 eggs, slightly beaten
1 tbsp. all-purpose flour
1/2 tsp. salt
1 1/4 cups palm sugar
1 tbsp. fried, thinly sliced shallot

PREPARATION :

1. In a mixing bowl, mix the coconut milk, flour and sugar well, Set aside.

2. In a separate bowl, mix the taro, eggs, and salt; beat until smooth.

3. Combine both mixtures in a pot and cook over medium heat for 5 minutes, then remove from heat.

4. Put this mixture in separate serving bowls, and bake in oven at 350°F. for 35 minutes, or until golden brown on top. Garnish with the fried shallots.

4 Serving

ส่วนผสม

เผือกสุกบดละเอียด 1 1/2 ถ้วย
กะทิ 1 1/4 ถ้วย
ไข่เป็ดตีให้เข้ากัน 5 ฟอง
แป้งสาลี 1 ช้อนโต๊ะ
เกลือ 1/2 ช้อนชา
น้ำตาลปีบ 1 1/4 ถ้วย
หอมแดงซอยทอดจนเป็นสีน้ำตาล 1 ช้อนโต๊ะ

วิธีทำ

๑. ผสมกะทิ แป้ง และน้ำตาลให้เข้ากันดี พักไว้

๒. ตีไข่ เผือกบด และเกลือให้เข้าเป็นเนื้อเดียวกันอย่างดี

๓. แล้วผสมทั้งสองส่วน คนให้เข้ากัน ตั้งไฟกลางประมาณ 5 นาที ยกลง

๔. ตักส่วนผสมใส่ถ้วย นำเข้าเตาอบ อบไฟ 350°ฟ ประมาณ 35 นาที หรือจนหน้าขนมเป็นสีน้ำตาล จึงโรยด้วยหอมเจียว

MAN CHEUAM
(Candied Sweet Potato)
มันเชื่อม

INGREDIENTS :

500 grams large sweet potatoes
1 1/2 cups sugar
2 cups water
1 1/2 cups limewater

PREPARATION :

1. Wash the sweet potatoes well and peel them. Cut them into pieces about 3/4 - inch thick. (If the sweet potatoes are small, slice them lengthwise; if large, slice across into discs.) Soak the sweet potato in limewater about half an hour and then wash in clean water before candying.

2. Place 2 cups water in a sauce pan or a wok and heat. When the water is hot, add the sugar and stir until it dissolves. If necessary, filter the solution to remove foreign matter.

3. Now bring the sugar solution to a boil in a wok. Allow to boil about five minutes and then add the sweet potatoes. The sweet potatoes need not be stirred often; they should, however, be turned from time to time. Reduce the heat as the syrup thickens and continue cooking until the syrup penetrates the potato completely.

4 Serving

MAN TOM NAM TAN
(Sweet Potatoes in Syrup)
มันต้มน้ำตาล

INGREDIENTS :

500 grams sweet potatoes
1 cup sugar
4-5 slices mature ginger

PREPARATION :

1. Peel the sweet potatoes, wash well, and slice them across into discs about one inch thick. Cut each disc into 4-6 wedges and soak in water.

2. Bring 4 cups water to a boil, add the sweet potato. When the pot comes to a boil once again, add the ginger and cook until the potato is tender. Then, add the sugar and leave on the heat until all the sugar has dissolved and the pot has returned to a good boil, then remove from heat.

4 Serving

ส่วนผสม

มันเทศหัวใหญ่ 500 กรัม
น้ำตาลทราย 1 1/2 ถ้วย
น้ำ 2 ถ้วย
น้ำปูนใส 1 1/2 ถ้วย

วิธีทำ

1. ล้างมันเทศให้สะอาด ปอกเปลือก หั่นเป็นชิ้นหนาประมาณ 3/4 นิ้ว (ถ้าหัวเล็กผ่าตามยาว ถ้าหัวใหญ่ให้ผ่าเป็นแว่น) แช่น้ำปูนใสประมาณ 1/2 ชั่วโมง ก่อนเชื่อมล้างน้ำอีกครั้ง

2. ใส่น้ำ 2 ถ้วยในกระทะทองเหลืองตั้งไฟ เมื่อน้ำร้อนเติมน้ำตาลคนจน น้ำตาลละลายหมด ยกลงกรองเอาผงออก

3. เทน้ำเชื่อมกลับใส่กระทะยกขึ้นตั้งไฟใหม่อีกประมาณ 5 นาที ใส่มันเทศ ลงเชื่อม (อย่าคนบ่อย) พลิกกลับชิ้นมันบ้าง พอน้ำตาลเริ่มข้น และซึมเข้า ชิ้นมัน จนชิ้นมันใส ตักขึ้น

ส่วนผสม

มันเทศ 500 กรัม
น้ำตาลทราย 1 ถ้วย
ขิงแก่ 4-5 แว่น

วิธีทำ

1. มันเทศปอกเปลือก ล้างสะอาด หั่นแว่น หนาประมาณ 1 นิ้ว ผ่า 4-6 ชิ้น ขนาดพอคำแช่น้ำไว้

2. ใส่น้ำ 4 ถ้วย ตั้งไฟพอเดือดใส่มันเทศ พอเดือดอีกครั้งใส่ขิง ต้มไปให้ มันสุกดี ใส่น้ำตาลทราย น้ำตาลละลายเดือดทั่วดี ยกลง

AISA-KHRIM KA-THI
(Coconut Milk Ice Cream)
ไอศกรีมกะทิ

INGREDIENTS :

3 1/2 cups coconut milk
1 cup sugar
1/2 cup water

PREPARATION :

1. Place the sugar and water in a pot and heat until the sugar dissolves. If necessary, filter the solution through cheesecloth to remove any foreign matter and then return to the heat. Continue heating to obtain a syrup thick enough to stick to a wooden paddle; then, remove from the heat.

2. When the syrup has cooled somewhat but is still warm, add the coconut milk and stir to mix well.

3. Pour the solution into an ice cream freezer and crank about 45 minutes, or until stiff. Coconut milk ice cream must be kept cold because it melts rapidly.

Note: freshly squeezed coconut milk will make the best ice cream.

6 *Serving*

ส่วนผสม

กะทิ 3 1/2 ถ้วย
น้ำตาลทราย 1 ถ้วย
น้ำสุก 1/2 ถ้วย

วิธีทำ

1. ใส่น้ำตาลและน้ำลงในหม้อและตั้งไฟจนน้ำตาลละลายหมด ยกลง กรองเศษผงออก และเทกลับใส่ในหม้อ ตั้งไฟต่อจนน้ำเชื่อมข้น ปิดไฟยกลง

2. เมื่อน้ำเชื่อมอุ่น ใส่หัวกะทิคนจนเข้ากันดี

3. เทส่วนผสมลงในถังปั่นไอกรีม ปั่นประมาณ 45 นาที หรือจนส่วนผสม แข็งตัว นำเข้าเก็บในช่องแช่แข็งของตู้เย็น เพราะถ้าทิ้งไว้จะละลาย หมายเหตุ หัวกะทิที่ใช้ทำไอศกรีมชนิดนี้ควรสด คั้นใหม่ ๆ

KAFAE YEN OR CHA YEN
(Thai-Style Iced Coffee or Tea)
กาแฟเย็น หรือ ชาเย็น

INGREDIENTS :

2 tbsp. ground coffee or powdered Thai tea leaves
1 1/2 cups boiling water
4 tbsp. sugar
1/4 cup unsweetened condensed milk
crushed ice or ice cubes

PREPARATION :

1. Place ground coffee or powered tea leaves in a cloth bag.

2. Place bag in a mug and pour the boiling water into the bag. Allow to steep a few moments, lift bag to a second mug, pour contents of the first mug into the bag, and repeat until desired strength is reached.

3. Remove bag, add sugar and milk, stir until dissolved, and pour into icefilled glasses.

2 Serving

ส่วนผสม

กาแฟคั่วบดหรือชาผงอย่างละ 2 ช้อนโต๊ะ
น้ำเดือด 1 1/2 ถ้วย
น้ำตาลทราย 4 ช้อนโต๊ะ
นมข้นจืด 1/4 ถ้วย
น้ำแข็งทุบหรือไอซ์คิ้วบ์

วิธีทำ

1. ใส่กาแฟหรือชาในถุงผ้าที่ใช้สำหรับกาแฟหรือชา

2. เอาถุงกาแฟใส่ไว้ในกระป๋องชง เทน้ำร้อนใส่ถุงกาแฟ แล้วยกถุงขึ้นมาพักในกระป๋องชงกาแฟอีกกระป๋องหนึ่ง เทน้ำกาแฟในกระป๋องแรกใส่ลงในถุงกาแฟยังอีกกระป๋องหนึ่งอีกครั้ง แล้วยกถุงกาแฟขึ้นพักไว้ยังกระป๋องที่ว่าง ทำเช่นนี้กลับไปกลับมาอีกสักสองสามครั้ง เพื่อให้ได้น้ำกาแฟเข้มข้นตามที่ต้องการ

3. เทน้ำกาแฟใส่ในแก้ว ชงน้ำตาล และนมข้นจืดให้เข้ากัน เทใส่แก้วที่เตรียมน้ำแข็งไว้แล้ว เสิร์ฟได้ 2 ที่

ABOUT THE AUTHER

Sisamon Kongpan has written ten books on the art of Thai cooking. As the reader will surmise, her menus and comments are pervasive with both the aesthetic and scientific. She has taught in the Faculty of Home Economics Rajamangala Insutitute of Technology, also in Bangkok. She studied at the University of Hawaii, after which she had become a professor of home economics at the above institute.

After teaching for 30 years, Sisamon is in a great demand, not only from the academic community, but from food industry as well. Her numerous workshops, courses, books, and other presentations have certainly earned her the title on the contemporary matriarch of Thai cuisine.

Much of the flavor of Sisamon's cookery comes from her upbringing in Chiang Rai Province in Northern Thailand with its own unique culture. Sisamon has synthesized her technical, artistic, and cultural background into an appealing method of teaching and writing. Concerned with her own Thai culture as well as Euroamerican influences, she is able to give us a presentation that is both instructive and crossculturally edifying.

Sangdad Publishing Co., Ltd.
320 Lat Phroa 94 (Town in Town), Wangthonglang, Bangkok 10310 Thailand
Tel. (662) 538-7576, 538-5553, 538-1499 Fax : (662) 538-1499
Printed in Thailand